Enhancing Independent Problem Solving in Mathematics

Enhancing Independent Problem Solving in Mathematics

Activities That Teach Problem Solving, Graphing, Charting, and Measurement Skills

 Routledge

Taylor & Francis Group

NEW YORK AND LONDON

Wayne P. Hresko, Ph.D. & Shelley R. Herron, Ph.D.

First published 1999 by Prufrock Press Inc.

Published 2021 by Routledge
605 Third Avenue, New York, NY 10017
2 Park Square, Milton Park, Abingdon, Oxon OX14 4RN

Routledge is an imprint of the Taylor & Francis Group, an informa business

ISBN 13: 978-1-59363-023-2 (pbk)

Table of Contents

Table of Contents

Introduction

Enhancing Independent Problem Solving in Mathematics is designed to work effectively with students of varying learning abilities. The activities have been designed for students in grades 3 through 5.

For many students, the lessons can be largely self-directing. The lessons can also be self-correcting at the option of the teacher by reproducing the answers found at the back of the *Teacher's Guide*. The directions are clear and easy for most students to follow. To assist the teacher, the skill being taught is named at the bottom of each lesson page. The subskill, which identifies for the student the purpose of a particular lesson, is found at the top of the page as the lesson's title. Whenever a new or variation of a subskill is introduced, the lesson is started with an example for the student. Frequent assists of this type allow the lessons to be self-directing for many students.

Features of the Activities
- Flexible in design and ease of use
- Self-directed when appropriate
- Self-corrected when appropriate
- Self-paced
- Teacher-directed when appropriate
- Directions are clear and easy to follow
- Adaptable for different instructional methods: for students working alone, cooperative learning teams, teacher-directed instruction

Cooperative Learning Teams

Cooperative learning procedures are particularly useful with the activities in these books. The majority of students in a regular classroom are able to work productively in a cooperative learning setting. Research shows that students of like ability working together in small skills teams or pairs learn well from each other. Cooperative learning enhances students' ability to follow directions, be self-directing, and independently proofread their own work.

The following guidelines should prove useful:
1. Always pair students of like ability.
2. It is important for students who have not worked in this type of setting to get off to a good start.
3. Begin with the group of children who make up the "most able" readers. Arrange students in pairs of like ability. At times, you may have an uneven amount of children, making it necessary to form a cooperative team of three. Assign to that team only students who work well with others.
   a. Each pair of students reads the directions to each other and discusses what to do. Demonstrate this procedure beforehand.

b. When the pairs (or threesome) understand what they are to do, they separate and each does his or her own work. When the members of the team have completed the page, they get together and compare their answers. If they both have the same answers, the team members explain to each other how they got their answer. Usually, this is sufficient. In the case of continued disagreement, the answers should be discussed with the teacher. Finally the pair checks its answers against the *Teacher's Guide*.

General Cooperative Learning Procedures

Read the instructions to your students before they begin working together. Each student should have a copy of the procedures on his or her page.

When the teachers want students to work cooperatively but don't want them correcting their own work, they should correct students' work directly with them.

From time to time, less able students following a directed-teaching lesson will benefit by doing a series of exercises with a partner. These teams should be temporary and followed immediately by teacher correction.

To the Student

1. Read the directions carefully. Then discuss with your partner what the directions ask you to do.
2. Separate and try to solve each exercise by yourself.
3. Compare your answers with your partner. If you both have the same answer, you are both probably correct. If your answers are different, one of you is probably wrong. By explaining to each other how you got your answer, it usually becomes clear which one of you is correct.
4. Mark the answers you cannot agree on.
5. Check your answers together against the answer guide. Carefully check the marked answers and circle the one that is correct. The person who had the correct answer should explain again how he or she go it.
6. In the case where both had the same answer and the same answer is wrong, work together to see how the correct answer was achieved.

Notes to the Teacher

At the beginning of new sections, you will find comments regarding the activities. As you read them, do the particular activity or group of activities yourself. Note any difficult or other items you will want to stress. This will assist you when the students working independently or in cooperative pairs need your help.

The problem solving process is basically simple. It encompasses the following steps:

1. Know where you are.
2. Know where you want to go.
3. Develop a strategy.
4. Implement it.
5. Arrive at a conclusion.
6. Check your answer.

The lessons in this book closely parallel these problem solving steps. At the third-grade level, it is as important to teach the problem solving *process* as it is to challenge and instruct the child in various *strategies*. The book, therefore, is organized to provide a logical progression in the acquisition of problem solving fluency rather than by mathematical function (addition, subtraction, etc.). The mathematics involved, however, progresses through the third-grade year, from easier to more difficult. These lessons can be used to supplement this curriculum or as discrete activities.

Providing for Students Who Are Gifted

Enhancing Independent Problem Solving in Mathematics: Activities That Teach Problem Solving, Graphing, Charting, and Measurement Skills is a math activity book that goes beyond the rote and literal level thinking of students. The activities challenge students to use critical, analytical, and divergent problem solving skills. The activities in the book provide students the opportunity to become actively engaged in synthesizing information and risk taking. These activities are ideal for students who are gifted. The activities encourage curiosity in students, which is the igniting spark that sets off asking questions, speculating hypothesis, and exploring different procedures and methods. Students who are gifted thrive on this type of process-orientated approach.

- **Lessons 1–4** deal with "Understanding the Question." A clear understanding of what is being asked for is critical to the problem solving process. The importance of this step should be emphasized to the student.

  In small groups or individually, have students write their own story problems with the missing question. Have other students determine the question and answer. Students should then self-evaluate their story problems and then other students' stories.

- **Lessons 5–11** are concerned with "Understanding What is Given." Students are asked to underline key facts, list key facts, and find missing facts. Special attention is given to the wording of problems introducing mathematical words and phrases to familiarize the student with the language of mathematics.

  In a small group, have students develop a "Missing Fact Card Game." Each student writes a story problem and cuts out the facts. The game is played similarly to "Go Fish." The objective of the game is to collect all the facts of one story problem. The students determine the rules of the game.

So, the first 11 lessons emphasize "Know where you are" and "Know where you want to go," the first two steps of the problem solving process. It remains now to find out "How to get there."

- At this point, the lessons of the book being to explore and develop strategies to solve problems. Illustrations, tables, analogies, and deductive reasoning are included in **Lessons 12–21.**

  Have students determine their own analogies based upon the lessons. Emphasize flexible thinking when determining the answer to the analogies. Discuss and debate why incorrect answers would not fit certain analogies.

- **Lessons 22–23** deal with estimation. One cannot underestimate the importance of this skill. With the mass availability of the computer, more and more of us will be looking at answers and printouts without access to the processes used to generate the answers. We have to be able to estimate or approximate the correct answer. Hence, checking the reasonability of the answer will be a skill of the 21st century (**Lesson 24**).

Have students determine their own estimation problems and then have students discuss the reasonableness of their estimations. Use self-evaluation techniques when determining the correct answer after the estimation exercise.

- **Lessons 25–27** concern "Concepts of Whole Number Operations." Whole number computation, measurement, number sense, and numeration are all reinforced throughout the book, but are emphasized in **Lessons 26 and 27** where students actually begin to do problems.

Have the students draw pictures that match the story problems to emphasize creativity and imagination when solving problems.

In **Lesson 28**, we begin introducing geometry with its figures and vocabulary in preparation of problems to come.

Have the students create designs using tanagrams or colored blocks to emphasize three dimensional abstract thinking.

The point of **Lessons 29** and **30** is to expose the students at an early age to the *Gestalt* school or problem solving thought. It helps students look at the overall picture, observe a pattern, and zero in on an elegant solution. Mathematics is full of patterns; it is advantageous to the student to be able to think *Gestalt*. It is also an invaluable process in generalizations.

Have the students create their own "Learning to Add Numbers Efficiently" activity sheet. Discuss why this is an important skill in life.

- **Lessons 31–41** are devoted to an analysis of the factual information given in various types of problems. No one can develop good problem solving strategies without first learning how to read and understand what the problem says. Once the student understands *what is given*, and, by extension, knows *what the question is*, it remains to develop strategies to arrive at an answer.

Have the students write a story problem with an answer and without facts. In small groups, exchange story problems and create the facts that would fit the answer.

- **Lessons 42–48** discuss such strategies as using charts, graphs, diagrams, and other illustrations to solve problems, as well as making tables and reading maps.

  Have the students use a real map to determine questions. Have the students draw a map of their neighborhood to determine questions.

- Other problem solving skills, such as the ability to estimate, predict round numbers, make comparisons and, and, and look for patterns, work efficiently—and a plethora of other strategies embedded in the problems discussed in the *Teacher's Guide* will be found in **Lessons 49–60**.

  Discuss various conclusions, comparisons, and reasonable answers in the presented activities. Use reciprocal teaching which involves the students acting as teachers to guide the discussion.

  Mathematical vocabulary permeates every lessons. It has been our experience that one reason students may not be better problem solvers is because they fail to understand the mathematical language in which the problems are written. A very conscious attempt has been made to remedy this situation. This problem solving series aims to expose the student not only to a wide variety of activities to abet critical and creative thinking, but also to the mathematical language necessary for successful continuing work in this discipline.

The activities in **Lessons 61–90** are written to supplement and lengthen any standard curriculum at the fifth grade level. They expose the student to an exciting diversity of problems and strategies that will stimulate the students' imagination and enhance problem solving ability across the curriculum. These activities are written conceptually and advance the guidelines of the recently published *Curriculum and Evaluation Standards for School Mathematics* by the National Council of the Teachers of Mathematics.

The activities are written in a problem solving format, introducing important techniques and strategies that reflect present emphases. "Guess and Test Techniques" (**Lessons 73–76**), "Pattern Recognition" (**Lessons 77–80**), "Geometric techniques" (**Lessons 81–82**) and "Thinking Ahead" (**Lesson 90**) are all discussed in a variety of problems and contexts. They take the student out of the reproductive mode and into a productive one.

Additionally, important subskills of problem solving permeate the text: ratios, combinations, open sentences reinforcing number sense, numerations, and whole and fractional number operations. **Lessons 67–74** and **83** introduce a plethora of charts and graphs, exposing the student to multiple techniques for organizing and representing data. Elementary statistics and probability are introduced to analyze numerical data, which is ever more prevalent in our society.

Providing for Students Who Are Gifted *(Cont.)*

Deductive reasoning, implication, converse, and logic in general are featured throughout the book in various practical contexts. The application of clear, organized, logical thought to solving problems and process information is an essential cross-disciplinary skill.

Detailed answers to the activities are given, along with generous comments on how best to present the material in class. A substantial effort is made to introduce mathematical notation and language. One cannot solve problems unless one understands the language, in which they are written.

Throughout these activities, have students use their creativity by drawing diagrams, models, and pictures to determine the most reasonable answer. The emphasis throughout these lessons should be the process of determining how to arrive at the answer versus the answer itself.

Providing for Students with Learning Differences

Students in a regular, heterogeneous classroom are usually grouped by ability in reading and language arts. The achieving students can usually work independently, either alone or in a cooperative learning team. These students tend to see more purpose in their work and find more transfer and application when they are able to immediately correct their own work. Working independently does not mean that these students, no matter how able, should be ignored or allowed to go their own way. The teacher must periodically circulate among the students working independently and ask individual students or teams to explain what they are doing, how they arrived at certain answers, or how they can apply what they are learning to their other assignments. Another suggestion is to create an index card with the word *help* written on it for each student or pair of students. When students or teams display the card, the teacher is able to notice easily those needing assistance. The above strategies, which use coaching techniques, encourage students to transfer skills they have learned to other areas of the curriculum.

Direct instruction by the teacher is essential for the less achieving student in the regular classroom—the student who is not sure what is to be done or does not understand how to do it. Allowing most of the students to work independently provides time for this task. Students experiencing learning differences and those with limited English language proficiency also benefit from teacher-directed instruction.

NCTM National Standards

The late 1980s and 1990s have seen the explosion of new thinking related to mathematical problem solving. During this time, several paradigms converged to give new direction to the field of mathematics education and to the education of children with gifted abilities. Central among these converging paradigms is that of constructivism and authentic learning.

Constructivism rejects the behavioral, reductionist arguments that lead to meaningless drill and isolated skill development. Authentic learning focuses on making instruction meaningful to the student by placing instruction in the context. As Rivera (1997) notes, this paradigmatic shift from predominantly reductionistic, skills-based instruction to a constructivist epistemology encompasses active student learning rooted in problem solving situations facilitated by teachers' guidance and questioning (p. 4). Thus, the emphasis has shifted from what appeared to be a pure skills-based approach to a more meaning, application-based approach.

In keeping with this view of learning within meaningful contexts, *Enhancing Independent Problem Solving in Mathematics* has taken problems from actual types of situations that a child might encounter. Rather than limit the child to solving story-based mathematical problems, we have included a variety of formats, including charts, graphs, pattern recognition, probability, measurement, estimation, and so forth. Since these problems require children to think through and resolve problems, the child uses more than rudimentary skills to achieve the solution. Such problems are especially useful for those advanced children who need more challenging educational opportunities. Children need not work on these problems in isolation. Teams, pairs, or small groups may be used for activities. Pairing advanced with less-able students may provide situations for cooperative learning to occur.

Each of the activities of *Enhancing Independent Problem Solving in Mathematics* conforms to one or more of the **Curriculum and Evaluation Standards for School Mathematics** as copyrighted by the National Council of Teachers of Mathematics (1989). A copy of these standards is included.

References

National Council of Teachers of Mathematics (1989). *Curriculum and evaluation standards for school mathematics*. Reston, VA: Author.

Rivera, D. P. (1997). Mathematics education and students with learning disabilities: Introduction to the special series. *Journal of Learning Disabilities*, 30(1), 2–19.

TABLE 1
NCTM Standards

Grades K–4

Standard 1: Mathematics as Problem Solving
- Use problem-solving approaches to investigate and understand mathematical content.
- Formulate problems from everyday and mathematical situations.
- Develop and apply strategies to solve a wide variety of problems.
- Verify and interpret results with respect to the original problem.
- Acquire confidence in using mathematics meaningfully.

Standard 2: Mathematics as Communication
- Relate physical materials, pictures, and diagrams to mathematical ideas.
- Reflect on and clarify their thinking about mathematical ideas and situations.
- Relate their everyday language to mathematical language and symbols.
- Realize that representing, discussing, reading, writing, and listening to mathematics are a vital part of learning and using mathematics.

Standard 3: Mathematics as Reasoning
- Draw logical conclusions about mathematics
- Use models, known facts, properties, and relationships to explain their thinking.
- Justify their answers and solution processes.
- Use patterns and relationships to analyze mathematical situations.
- Believe that mathematics makes sense.

Standard 4: Mathematical Connections
- Link conceptual and procedural knowledge.
- Relate various representations of concepts or procedures to one another.
- Recognize relationships among different topics in mathematics.
- Use mathematics in other curriculum areas.
- Use mathematics in their daily lives.

Standard 5: Estimation
- Explore estimation strategies.
- Recognize when an estimate is appropriate.
- Determine the reasonableness of results.
- Apply estimation in working with quantities, measurement, computation, and problem solving.

Standard 6: Number Sense and Numeration
- Construct number meanings through real-world experiences and the use of physical materials.
- Understand our numeration system by relating counting, grouping, and place-value concepts.
- Develop number sense.
- Interpret the multiple uses of numbers encountered in the real world.

Standard 7: Concepts of Whole Number Operations
- Develop meaning for the operations by modeling and discussing a rich variety of problem situations.
- Relate the mathematical language and symbolism of operations to problem situations and informal language.
- Recognize that a wide variety of problem structures can be represented by a single operation.
- Develop operation sense.

Standard 8: Whole Number Computation
- Model, explain, and develop reasonable proficiency with basic facts and algorithms.
- Use a variety of mental computation and estimation techniques.
- Use calculators in appropriate computational situations.
- Select and use computation techniques appropriate to specific problems and determine whether the results are reasonable.

Standard 9: Geometry and Spatial Sense
- Describe, model, draw, and classify shapes.
- Investigate and predict the results of combining, subdividing, and changing shapes.
- Develop spatial sense.
- Relate geometric ideas to number and measurement ideas.
- Recognize and appreciate geometry in their world.

Standard 10: Measurement
- Understand the attributes of length, capacity, weight, mass, area, volume, time, temperature, and angle.
- Develop the process of measuring and concepts related to units of measurement.
- Make and use estimates of measurement.
- Make and use measurements in problem and everyday situations.

Standard 11: Statistics and Probability
- Collect, organize, and describe data.
- Construct, read, and interpret displays of data.
- Formulate and solve problems that involve collecting and analyzing data.
- Explore concepts of chance.

Standard 12: Fractions and Decimals
- Develop concepts of fractions, mixed numbers, and decimals.
- Develop number sense for fractions and decimals.
- Use models to relate fractions to decimals and to find equivalent fractions.
- Use models to explore operations on fractions and decimals.
- Apply fractions and decimals to problem situations.

Standard 13: Patterns and Relationships
- Recognize, describe, extend, and create a wide variety of patterns.
- Represent and describe mathematical relationships.
- Explore the use of variables and open sentences to express relationships.

Grades 5–8

Standard 1: Mathematics as Problem Solving
- Use problem-solving approaches to investigate and understand mathematical concepts.
- Formulate problems from situations within and outside mathematics.
- Develop and apply a variety of strategies to solve problems, with emphasis on multistep and nonroutine problems.
- Verify and interpret results with respect to the original problem situation.
- Generalize solutions and strategies to new problem situations.
- Acquire confidence in using mathematics meaningfully.

Standard 2: Mathematics as Communication
- Model situations using oral, written, concrete, pictorial, graphical, and algebraic methods.
- Reflect on and clarify their own thinking about mathematical ideas and situations.
- Develop common understandings of mathematical ideas, including the role of definitions.
- Use the skills of reading, listening, and viewing to interpret and evaluate mathematical ideas.
- Discuss mathematical ideas and make conjectures and convincing arguments.
- Appreciate the value of mathematical notation and its role in the development of mathematical ideas.

Standard 3: Mathematics as Reasoning
- Recognize and apply deductive and inductive reasoning.

- Understand and apply reasoning processes, with special attention to spatial reasoning and reasoning with proportions and graphs.
- Make and evaluate mathematical conjectures and arguments.
- Validate their own thinking.
- Appreciate the pervasive use and power of reasoning as a part of mathematics.

Standard 4: Mathematical Connections
- See mathematics as an integrated whole.
- Explore problems and describe results using graphical, numerical, physical, algebraic, and verbal mathematical models or representations.
- Use a mathematical idea to further their understanding of other mathematical ideas.
- Apply mathematical thinking and modeling to solve problems that arise in other disciplines, such as art, music, psychology, science, and business.
- Value the role of mathematics in our culture and society.

Standard 5: Number and Number Relationships
- Understand, represent, and use numbers in a variety of equivalent forms (integer, fraction, decimal, percentage, exponential, and scientific notation) in real-world and mathematical problems.
- Develop number sense for whole numbers, fractions, decimals, integers, and rational numbers.
- Understand and apply ratios, proportions, percentages in a wide variety of situations.
- Investigate relationships among fractions, decimals, and percentages.
- Represent numerical relationships in one- and two-dimensional graphs.

Standard 6: Number Systems and Number Theory
- Understand and appreciate the need for numbers beyond the whole numbers.
- Develop and use order relations for whole numbers, fractions, decimals, integers, and rational numbers.
- Extend their understanding of whole number operations to fractions, decimals, integers, and rational numbers.
- Understand how the basic arithmetic operations are related to one another.
- Develop and apply number theory concepts (e.g., primes, factors, and multiples) in real-world and mathematical problem situations.

Standard 7: Computation and Estimation
- Compute with whole numbers, fractions, decimals, integers, and rational numbers.
- Develop, analyze, and explain procedures for computation and techniques for estimation.
- Develop, analyze, and explain methods for solving proportions.
- Select and use an appropriate method for computing from among mental computation, paper-and-pencil, calculator, and computer methods.
- Use computation, estimation, and proportions to solve problems.
- Use estimation to check the reasonableness of results.

Standard 8: Patterns and Functions
- Describe, extend, analyze, and create a wide variety of patterns.
- Describe and represent relationships with tables, graphs, and rules.
- Analyze functional relationships to explain how a change in one quantity results in a change in another.
- Use patterns and functions to represent and solve problems.

Standard 9: Algebra
- Understand the concepts of variable, expression, and equation.
- Represent situations and number patterns with tables, graphs, verbal rules, and equations and explore the interrelationships of these representations.
- Analyze tables and graphs to identify properties and relationships.

- Develop confidence in solving linear equations using concrete, informal, and formal methods.
- Investigate inequalities and nonlinear equations informally.
- Apply algebraic methods to solve a variety of real-world and mathematical problems.

Standard 10: Statistics
- Systematically collect, organize, and describe data.
- Construct, read, and interpret tables, charts, and graphs.
- Make inferences and convincing arguments that are based on data analysis.
- Evaluate arguments that are based on data analysis
- Develop an appreciation for statistical methods as powerful means for decision making.

Standard 11: Probability
- Model situations by devising and carrying out experiments or simulations to determine probabilities.
- Model situations by constructing a sample space to determine probabilities.
- Appreciate the power of using a probability model by comparing experimental results with mathematical expectations.
- Make predictions that are based on experimental or theoretical probabilities.
- Develop an appreciation for the pervasive use of probability in the real world.

Standard 12: Geometry
- Identify, describe, compare, and classify geometric figures.
- Visualize and represent geometric figures with special attention to developing spatial sense.
- Explore transformations of geometric figures.
- Represent and solve problems using geometric models.
- Understand and apply geometric properties and relationships.
- Develop an appreciation of geometry as a means of describing the physical world.

Standard 13: Measurement
- Extend their understanding of the process of measurement.
- Estimate, make, and use measurements to describe and compare phenomena.
- Select appropriate units and tools to measure to the degree of accuracy required in a particular situation.

Grades 9–12

Standard 1: Mathematics as Problem Solving
- Use, with increasing confidence, problem-solving approaches to investigate and understand mathematical content.
- Apply integrated mathematical problem-solving strategies to solve problems from within and outside mathematics.
- Recognize and formulate problems from situations within and outside mathematics.
- Apply the process of mathematical modeling to real-world problem situations.

Standard 2: Mathematics as Communication
- Reflect upon and clarify their thinking about mathematical ideas and relationships.
- Formulate mathematical definitions and express generalizations discovered through investigations.
- Express mathematical ideas orally and in writing.
- Read written presentations of mathematics with understanding.
- Ask clarifying and extending questions related to mathematics they have read or heard about.
- Appreciate the economy, power, and elegance of mathematical notation and its role in the development of mathematical ideas.

Standard 3: Mathematics as Reasoning
- Make and test conjectures.
- Formulate counterexamples.
- Follow logical arguments.
- Judge the validity of arguments.
- Construct simple valid arguments.
  and so that, in addition, college-intending students can—

Book 1 • Grade 3

Facts & Information

Finding the Question

Directions: Underline the question in each paragraph.
The first one is done.

1. Mrs. Skills took eight boys and six girls to the playground. <u>How many</u> children did Mrs. Skills take <u>altogether</u>?

2. At the sporting goods store, a baseball costs $4.00. Leo has saved $2.75. How much more money does Leo need to buy the baseball?

3. The Chase family plans a trip to the coast starting next Thursday morning. It is now Monday morning. How many more days before the Chase family leaves?

4. Tom is five years older than Jack. If Jack is six years old now, how old is Tom?

5. The train going to Philadelphia departs at 2:15 p.m. The trip takes two hours. What time will the train arrive in Philadelphia?

6. The Red Sox beat the Yankees 3–2 last night. Tom was smiling while Joe was unhappy. Who was the Red Sox fan?

7. I had some money and Mom gave me $5.00 more. Now I have $11.00. How much money did I have to start with?

8. Tom's house is seven miles west of the school. Leo's house is five miles north of the school. Who has the longer ride to school?

9. James counted four squares while Russell counted five. Who counted correctly?

10. The Giants were 6 points ahead of the Patriots at halftime. If the Giants had 14 points, what was the Patriots' point total at halftime?

2 — Choosing the Correct Question

Directions: Read the problem carefully. Then decide which sentence asks the same question as the problem asks. Circle its letter. The first one is done.

1. Find out how many games the Mustangs won if they played 12 games and lost 3.

    a. How many games did the Mustangs play?
    b. How many games did the Mustangs lose?
    (c.) How many games did the Mustangs win?

2. If I started out with $10.00 and spent all but $3.00, how much money did I spend?

    a. How much is $10.00 + $3.00?
    b. What is the difference between $10.00 and $3.00?
    c. How many things could I buy?

3. Joshua has two coins. They total $.11. What are they?

    a. What two coins total $.11?
    b. How much is 5 + 6?
    c. What do a dime and a nickel equal?

4. Detroit has about one million people. New York has a population of about eight million. About how many more people live in New York than in Detroit?

    a. What is Detroit's population?
    b. What is New York's population?
    c. What is the difference between the populations of New York and Detroit?

17

5. Is the area of a room that is 15 feet long and 12 feet wide bigger or smaller than 150 square feet?

    a. Is the room big?

    b. Is the size of the room more than or less than 150 square feet?

    c. Is 150 square feet equal to 15 feet x 12 feet?

Choosing the Correct Question

Directions: Circle the letter beside the question that is being asked.

1. Naomi spent $12.00 on a blouse, $6.00 on a calculator, and $.75 for a pen. How much money did she spend in all?

    a. What is the cost of the calculator?
    b. What is the total amount that Naomi spent?
    c. How much money did Naomi have left?

2. Find the weight of a 10-inch pizza with eight ounces of dough, two ounces of cheese, three ounces of pepperoni, and half a dozen mushrooms weighing one ounce.

    a. How much does everything weigh altogether?
    b. How much does a 10-inch pizza cost?
    c. How much pepperoni was on the pizza?

3. Charles walks three miles to school every day. Cornelia walks one mile to school. Jo walks five miles. How much farther does Jo walk than Charles?

    a. How far do the children walk to school?
    b. Who walks the farthest distance?
    c. What is the difference between five and three?

4. Nat saw 15 ducks swimming on the lake. Eight more flew up and joined them. Then four flew away. How many ducks were left?

    a. What does 15 + 8 - 4 equal?
    b. What is the total of 15 + 8 + 4?
    c. How many ducks flew away?

5. A square field with a length of 50 feet and a width of 50 feet has a square swimming pool. The pool is 30 feet by 30 feet. How much of the field is covered by grass?

    a. What is the area of the field?
    b. How large is the swimming pool?
    c. What is the area of the field that is not covered by the swimming pool?

Rewriting the Question

Directions: Find out what the problem is asking, then rewrite the question in your own words.

1. Andrew went to the grocery store. He picked up an apple and brought it to the cashier. Andrew gave the cashier $1.00. The cashier gave him back $.50. Why?

   The question is: _____

   _____?

2. In May and June, less than two inches of rain fell. July was the month the farmers were happy. Why?

Rainfall Chart

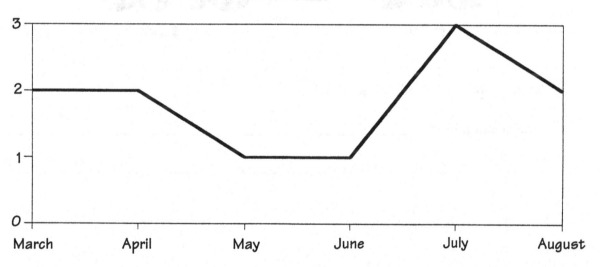

   The question is: _____

   _____?

3. There are three brothers in the Johnson family: Josh, Joseph, and James. The oldest brother is going to camp. Josh is 10 years old. Joseph is three years younger than Josh. James is four years older than Joseph. Who is going to camp?

The question is: _____

_____?

4.

SUPERSODA   TERRIFIC TONIC

$1.80 $1.80

More people buy Terrific Tonic. Why?

The question is: _____

_____?

Underlining and Listing Facts

Directions: In each paragraph, underline the number facts you will need to answer the questions. Then list them on the lines below.

1. Tom is seven years older than Bill. Bill is eight years old. How old is Tom?
   Facts: a. _____
   b. _____

2. Nina is building a play house. She needs $45.00 for boards, $5.00 for nails, and $15.00 for paint. How much money does she need to build the playhouse?
   Facts: a. _____
   b. _____
   c. _____

3. Alex is doing his homework. He has been given 15 problems and he has done eight. How many problems does he have left to do?
   Facts: a. _____
   b. _____

4. Jon went to the store and bought one pencil for $.59, two notebooks for $3.00 each, and an eraser for $.31. What was his total bill?
   Facts: a. _____
   b. _____
   c. _____

5. Sue and Maria worked on a job. Sue worked for two hours. Maria worked for one hour. They earned $12.00. If Sue's share was $8.00, what was Maria's share?
   Facts: a. _____
   b. _____

Underlining and Listing Facts

Direction: Underline all of the facts in each paragraph. Then list them on the lines below.

1. Leo wants to buy a baseball glove for $14.00. His allowance is $2.00 a week. For how many weeks will Leo have to save his allowance to buy the glove?
    Facts: a. _____
    b. _____

2. Phyllis had $10.00 in her bank. How much did she have after she saved $3.00 more, then spent $5.00?
    Facts: a. _____
    b. _____
    c. _____

3. Nancy wants to know if she has won a good-attendance award at school. She was absent only six times during the year. The award is given to children who have missed no more than one week of school. Will Nancy get an award?
    Facts: a. _____
    b. _____

4. Roger practices the piano for 30 minutes each day. Does Roger practice more than four hours a week?
    Fact: _____

5. A book has 48 pages. Jeremiah read 20 pages in 30 minutes. How many pages did Jeremiah not read?
    Facts: a. _____
    b. _____

Using Facts to Decide

Directions: Read the facts and then check (✔) what best completes the sentence. The first one is done.

Facts

1.
   1. She helps people.
   2. She is not a nurse.
   3. She does not work in a school.
   4. She works in a hospital.

2.
   1. We put on our sneakers.
   2. Mom got her camera.
   3. Dad needed his binoculars.
   4. The sea was rough.

3.
   1. Its shape is round.
   2. It does not have a hole in it.
   3. She does not use fruit.
   4. I like it with butter.

4.
   1. The weather is not hot.
   2. The leaves on the trees are falling.
   3. The season is not spring.
   4. The month has 31 days.

5.
   1. It does not have feathers.
   2. It has whiskers.
   3. It is a wonderful swimmer.
   4. It does not build dams.

Sentences

She has an appointment with a
___ (a) lawyer
✔ (b) doctor
___ (c) plumber
___ (d) teacher

Our family went
___ (a) bird watching
___ (b) hiking
___ (c) bicycling
___ (d) whale watching

Mrs. Hiroka makes very good
___ (a) doughnuts
___ (b) bread
___ (c) apple pie
___ (d) spaghetti

My birthday is in the middle of
___ (a) August
___ (b) September
___ (c) April
___ (d) October

Our favorite zoo animal is the
___ (a) ostrich
___ (b) beaver
___ (c) elephant
___ (d) seal

Directions: Use the facts in Nancy's schedule to answer the questions.

Nancy's Schedule

OCTOBER

S	M	T	W	TH	F	S
		1	2 MATH TEST	3	4 SPELLING TEST	5 SOCCER GAME 1 pm
6	7	8 LIBRARY	9	10	11 SPELLING TEST	12 SOCCER GAME 3 pm
13	14 HOLIDAY	15	16 MATH TEST	17 BOOK REPORT DUE	18 SPELLING TEST	19 SOCCER GAME 9 am
20	21	22 LIBRARY	23	24	25 SPELLING TEST	26 SOCCER GAME 2 pm
27	28	29 ½ DAY SCHOOL	30 MATH TEST	31		

Finding the Facts *(Cont.)*

1. a. On what day does Nancy have her spelling test? _____

    b. How often does she have a spelling test? _____

2. a. On what day will Nancy visit the library with her class? _____

    b. How often will Nancy visit the library? _____

3. What facts do you know about Nancy's math test schedule? _____

    _____

4. When will Nancy have three days off from school? _____

    _____

5. Nancy has a friend who wants her to visit on a Saturday afternoon. When can Nancy visit her friend?

    _____

6. Nancy needs two weeks to read her book for her report. When should she begin to read the book?

    _____

Finding the Facts

Directions: List the facts from the poster to answer the questions.

ANTIQUES & CRAFTS SHOW

Marshfield Fairgrounds
Sunday, October 10
Gates Open at 7:00 a.m.
Admission: Sellers - $15.00 per car space
Adults - $2.00
Children under 12 - Free

Sponsored by South Shore Rotary Club
Public Welcome

---

1. On what date will the event take place?

   _____

2. What kind of an event is it?

   _____

3. What time will it start?

   _____

4. Where will the event take place?

   _____

5.   George said that Tina could not go because she was not invited. Is George telling the truth?

   _____

6.   How much did the people who were selling crafts have to pay?

   _____

7.   Mr. Ford's third-grade class went to see the crafts. How much did he have to pay for the whole class?

   _____

8.   The person at the gate who was collecting the money was a member of what club?

   _____

9.   Mr. and Mrs. Costas took their 16-year-old daughter, Anita, and their 10-year-old son, George. How much did they pay

   a.   for Anita's ticket?   _____
   b.   for George's ticket?   _____
   c.   for Mr. Costa?   _____
   d.   for Mrs. Costa?   _____
   e.   altogether?   _____

10.   In the show, there was a woman who was making dolls out of pieces of leftover cloth. Was she in the antiques section or in the crafts section?

   _____

Getting the Right Answer from the Facts

Directions: Read the following problems carefully. Then make up your mind as to which answers are True, False, or ING (Information Not Given). Circle your answer.

1. The Cougars played the Lions last night in a game of baseball.
    The final score was Cougars 12 and Lions 9.

    a. The Lions won the game by three points.   T   F   ING
    b. The total number of runs scored was 21.   T   F   ING
    c. The game went to 10 innings.   T   F   ING
    d. On the Lions, Tom scored three runs, Dick five,
        and Jane four.   T   F   ING

2. At the local fruit stand, an apple costs $.50, an orange $.25, and a banana $.30.

    a. The apples were red.   T   F   ING
    b. Judy paid $1.10 for two bananas and an apple.   T   F   ING
    c. Andy bought two apples, three bananas, and
        an orange for $2.00.   T   F   ING
    d. Tom got $.20 back from $1.00 after buying
        an apple and a banana.   T   F   ING

3. Tom's go-cart has a two-gallon tank. It can travel for six miles on one gallon of gasoline.

    a. Tom can travel six miles per hour.   T   F   ING
    b. Tom can go 12 miles on a full tank.   T   F   ING
    c. Tom was wearing a safety belt.   T   F   ING
    d. Tom can complete a 14-mile track without
        stopping.   T   F   ING

4. A school has 10 teachers, eight classrooms, and 120 students

    a. There is a classroom for every teacher.   T   F   ING
    b. The school can form 10 teams with 11 players each.   T   F   ING
    c. Each classroom can have 15 students.   T   F   ING
    d. The school has 65 girls and 55 boys.   T   F   ING

5. Jane spends four hours in classes, one hour in sports, and 30 minutes listening to music each school day.

    a. Jane listens to music for three hours during the school week.   T   F   ING
    b. Jane plays soccer but not baseball.   T   F   ING
    c. Jane spends 20 hours in the classroom per week.   T   F   ING
    d. Jane spends two hours per night on homework.   T   F   ING

6. Brad and Nat were sorting their coin collections. Brad had four Indian head nickels, eight Kennedy half dollars, five Susan B. Anthony dollars, and a 1915 dime. Nat had coins from many different countries.

    a. Brad had $9.30 in coins.   T   F   ING
    b. Nat's collection was more valuable than Brad's.   T   F   ING
    c. Brad had four different kinds of coins.   T   F   ING
    d. Nat and Brad are brothers.   T   F   ING

7. Mary's pets are named Clover and Cassius. Cassius jumps on the ironing board so Mary can rub his back. Clover likes to sit in the window.

    a. Cassius is older than Clover is.   T   F   ING
    b. Clover likes to watch birds.   T   F   ING
    c. Cassius is a male.   T   F   ING
    d. Mary has three pet cats.   T   F   ING

Finding the Missing Fact

Directions: One more fact is needed before you can solve each problem. Read the problem. Then circle a, b, or c to show the missing fact. The first one is done.

1. Lauren has saved $5.00 and wants to buy a record. How much money will she have left?

    a. The store sells only books.
    b. Her allowance is $1.00 a week.
    c. The record costs $4.99.

2. Tom took his friend Paul to the movies. After paying for two tickets, he had $2.00 left. How much money did Tom start with?

    a. The movie started at 8 p.m.
    b. A ticket costs $4.00.
    c. Popcorn costs $1.00.

3. Margaret left home to go to the library at 6:30 p.m. How long did it take her to get there?

    a. The library is two miles away.
    b. She arrived there at 6:50 p.m.
    c. She left the library at 8 p.m.

4. Andrew has either a moth or a butterfly in his jar. How can Andrew tell if the insect is a moth or a butterfly?

    a. Both moths and butterflies have six legs.
    b. Only a moth has fuzzy antennas.
    c. Some moths like to eat wool rugs.

5. Helen rode her bike once around the block. The longer side of the block is 50 yards. How many yards did she travel?

    a. The shorter side of the block is 30 yards long.
    b. There is a path around the block.
    c. Helen got a flat tire.

6. Marie has two coins in her purse. One is a quarter. What is the other coin?

    a. Marie just received her allowance.
    b. Marie wants to buy an ice cream cone for $.30.
    c. Marie has $.35 in her purse.

7. Matthew is three years younger than his brother, Robert. How old is Matthew?

    a. Robert is three years older than Matthew.
    b. Matthew and Robert have an older brother who is 15.
    c. Robert is 12 years old.

8. On Arbor Day, 1988, we planted a tree in the schoolyard. If the tree grows about one foot per year, when will the tree be six feet tall?

    a. The tree is an evergreen.
    b. The tree is now three feet tall.
    c. There are 12 inches in one foot.

Book 2 • Grade 3

Problem Solving Strategies

Using Illustrations

1. **Directions: Read the problem.**

Erica placed three blocks on top of each other. One block was red, one was green, and one was yellow. She had stacked the blocks so that:

- the middle block was not green

- the block on top was yellow:

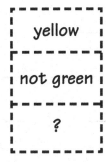

yellow

not green

?

Use the picture and the facts above to help you answer the questions.
a. Which block was on top of the stack? _____
b. Which block was in the middle? _____
c. Which block was on the bottom of the stack? _____

Use the answers to the questions to color each block:

2. **Directions: Cross out information not needed to solve the problem. Then answer the question.**

The temperature was 30° in the morning. It went up to 55° by noon. It went to 45° in the evening. What was the difference in temperature between morning and evening? _____

Using Illustrations: Graph

Directions: Use the graph to answer the following questions.

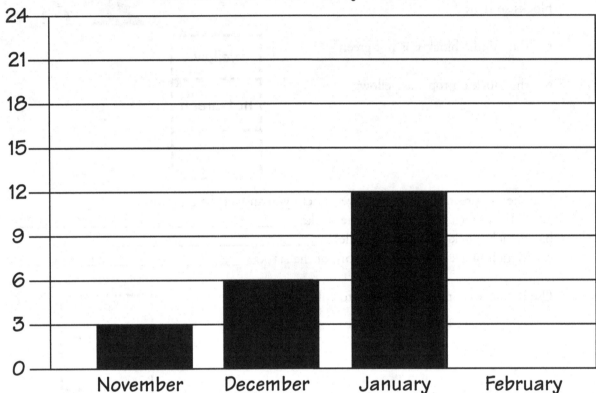

Snowfall in Inches for Rocky Mount, USA

1. Last year, the total snowfall for November through February was 30 inches. This year it was the same. How much snow fell in February? _____

   Fill in the graph for February.

2. Which month had the least snow? _____

3. How much snow must fall in February to double the amount that fell in January? _____

4. What was the total snowfall for November and January? _____

5. Which months had twice the amount of snow as the months that came before? _____

   _____

Using Illustrations: Chart

Directions: Use the chart below to answer the questions.

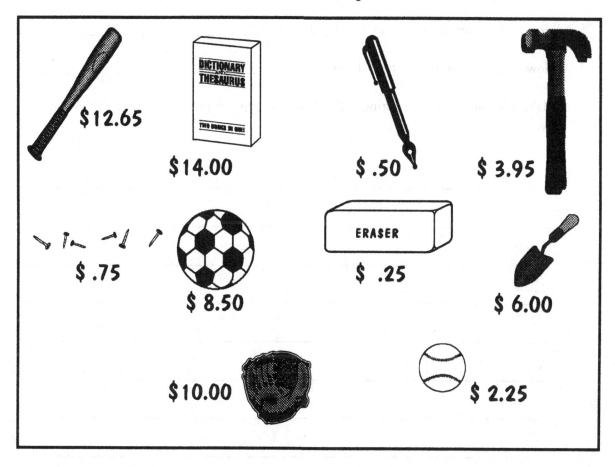

1. How many items cost more than $9.00? _____

2. How many items cost less than $5.00? _____

3. How many items cost over $1.00 but less than $7.00? _____

4. What is the difference in price between a pen and an eraser? _____

5. How many items cost between $3.00 and $6.50? _____

6. How many sports items are on the chart? _____

7. How many school items are on the chart? _____

8. Make a list of the items, starting with the *least* expensive and ending with the *most* expensive.

_____

_____

_____

_____

_____

_____

_____

_____

_____

_____

_____

Using Illustrations: Map

Directions: Use the map to answer the questions.

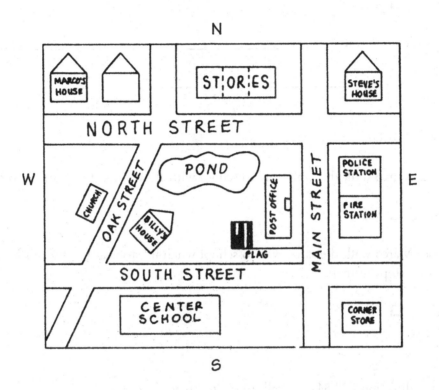

1. Use the map above to show which way Marco will go to school in each of the situations listed below.

   a. Marco needs to stop at the post office to mail some letters before going to school today. Draw his route on the map with a red crayon.

   b. Marco is going to walk to school with Billy today. He needs to stop at Billy's house to pick him up. Draw Marco's route on the map with a blue crayon.

   c. Marco is going to Steve's house before school today. Both of them are going to stop at the corner store and then go to school. Draw the route on the map with a green crayon.

   d. Marco is going to school by himself and not making any stops. Draw his route on the map with a yellow crayon.

2. Is there one single best way for Marco to walk to school every day?

    ❏ yes   ❏ no

    If yes, which one is it? _____

    _____

3. Test your answer:

    a. Does Marco walk the same way to school with Billy as he does with Steve?

    ❏ yes   ❏ no

    b. Does Marco walk the same way to school when he stops at the post office as when he has no stops to make?

    ❏ yes   ❏ no

4. In which direction will Marco walk to get to Steve's house? _____

5. Steve and Marco walk in which direction to school? _____

1. I started my walk at point A. If I walk four blocks east, two blocks north, two blocks west, and one block south, how many blocks away from A will I be? _____. Mark the block.

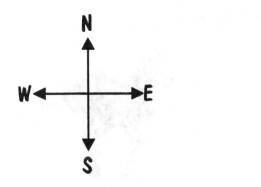

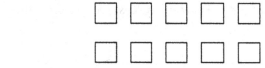

Point A •

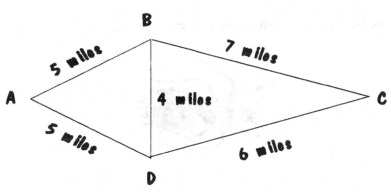

a. Color the path that will take you from A to C in 15 miles.

b. What is the shortest distance from A to C? _____

c. If you travel three miles from B toward C, how far are you from A? _____

d. How much fencing will you need to enclose triangle ABD? _____

e. What is the mileage of the path A-B-C-D-A? _____

Using Illustrations

1. How many hours between 1:30 p.m. and 8:30 p.m.? _____

    How many hours between 9 a.m. and 2:30 p.m.? _____

2. a. How many legs does a beetle and a horse have altogether? _____

    b. Who has more legs, this ant or the beetle? _____

    c. There are 24 ant legs. How many ants are there? _____

    d. There are three ants, two ducks, and two horses. How many legs are there in all? __

    e. There are 10 legs altogether. Who could they belong to?
        Circle the correct answer.

        i.   Beetle and horse.

        ii. Three ducks and a horse.

        iii. Two ants and a horse.

Using Analogies: Compare and Contrast

Directions: Choose the word that best completes the sentence. Write the word in the blank.

1. Arm is to hand as leg is to _____.
   foot   elbow   head

2. Night is to day as black is to _____.
   blue   white   green

3. Puppy is to dog as kitten is to _____.
   cow   cat   horse

4. Fur is to animal as feather is to _____.
   insect   bird   reptile   hat

5. Racquet is to tennis as _____ is to baseball.
   golf   net   stick   bat

6. _____ is to man as girl is to woman.
   brother   father   boy   sister

7. Shovel is to dig as needle is to _____.
   sew   iron   wash   cook

8. Day is to night as _____ is to dark.
   light   black   white   star

9. House is to people as _____ is to birds.
   tree   cave   nest   forest

10. Duckling is to duck as chick is to _____.
    eagle   hen   pig   cow

19

Using Analogies to Describe Change

Directions: See how the figures in the left column change. Then complete the second column the same way. The first one is done.

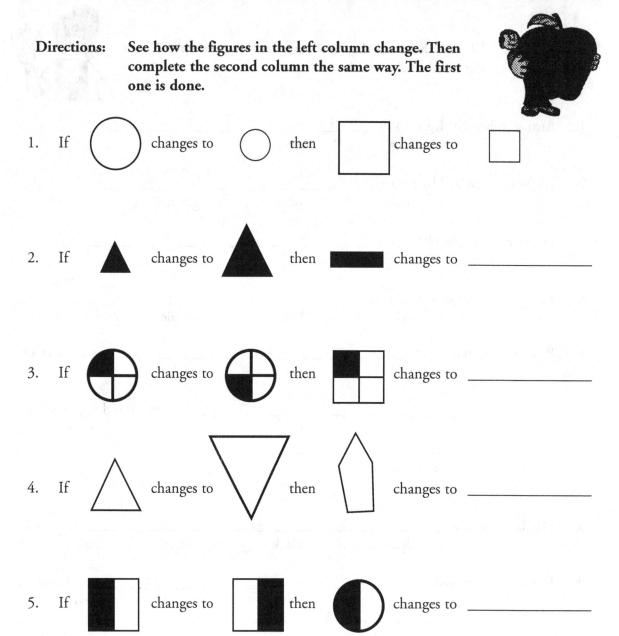

1. If ◯ changes to ◯ then ▢ changes to ▢

2. If ▲ changes to ▲ then ▬ changes to _____

3. If ⊕ changes to ⊕ then ⊞ changes to _____

4. If △ changes to ▽ then ⬠ changes to _____

5. If ◨ changes to ◨ then ◐ changes to _____

6. If ◇ changes to ◆ then ▭ changes to _____

7. If ▱ changes to ▱ then ◻ changes to _____

8. If ⬤ changes to ⬤ then ⬜ changes to _____

9. If **abc** changes to **cba** then **123** changes to _____

10. If **5 + 6** changes to **6 + 5** then **8 x 6** changes to _____

20

Using Analogies to Solve Problems

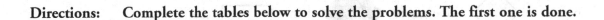

Directions: Complete the tables below to solve the problems. The first one is done.

1. If on one gallon of gas a car goes 10 miles, then on three gallons of gas the car will go _____ miles.

Complete this table for the car.

gallons of gas	1	2	3	4	5	6
miles	10	20	30	40	50	60

2. A heavy truck goes four miles on one gallon of gas. How much gas will the truck need to go 24 miles? _____

Complete this table for the truck.

gallons of gas	1	2	4	6	8
miles	4		16		

3. If one beehive produces six quarts of honey, then five beehives will produce _____ quarts of honey?

Complete this table for the beehives.

number of hives	1	3	5	7	9
jars of honey	6	18			

Using Analogies to Solve Problems *(Cont.)*

4. If James can walk one mile in 20 minutes, then he can walk _____ miles in 60 minutes.

Complete this table below for James.

miles	1	2	3	4	5	6
minutes	20					

5. Mrs. O'Keefe is planning a party for the Scouts. She made three cookies for each Scout. How many cookies does she need for 12 Scouts? _____

Complete this table below for Mrs. O'Keefe.

scouts	1	3	6	9	12	15
cookies	3					

6. If one out of every five tomatoes spoils during transport, how many tomatoes spoil in a box of 25? _____ Draw the table.

21

Using Logic to Solve Problems

A. 1. a. All cats have fur.
Hector is a cat.

Write the word from the box that makes the sentence true.

Hector has _____.

fingers	hair	fur

b. All cats have fur.
Hector is a skinny cat.
Hector likes to climb trees.

Question: Does Hector have fur? ❑ yes ❑ no
Underline the facts that show your answer is correct.
Circle the fact that does not help you.

2. a. All spiders have eight legs.
An octopus has eight legs.

Question: Is an octopus a spider? ❑ yes ❑ no

b. **Question: If an animal has eight legs
is it always a spider?** ❑ yes ❑ no

Why? _____

_____

_____

Using Logic to Solve Problems *(Cont.)*

Directions: Read the statements below. Then tell whether the conclusion is True or False. The first one is done.

B. 1.   Ellen owns a cat or a dog.
        She does not own a cat.

        Conclusion: Ellen owns a dog.
        _____True_____

2.   Tom lives in Boston.
     Boston is in Massachusetts.

     Conclusion: Tom lives in Massachusetts.
     _____

3.   Some people own Chevy trucks.
     Jose owns a truck.

     Conclusion: Jose owns a Chevy.
     _____

4.   All ducks can swim.
     Tina is a swimmer.

     Conclusion: Tina is a duck.
     _____

5.   All Dos are Maks.
     Tom is a Mak.

     Conclusion: Tom is a Dos.
     _____

6.   All triangles have three sides.
     ABC is a triangle.

     Conclusion: ABC has three sides.
     _____

7.   All lions are wild.
     Ginger is wild.

     Conclusion: Ginger is a lion.
     _____

8.   Some cows are black.
     Gordon owns a cow.

     Conclusion: Gordon's cow is black.
     _____

9.   Jane is in history or in music.
     She is not in music.

     Conclusion: Jane plays the flute.
     _____

10. All squares are rectangles.
     ABCD is a rectangle.

     Conclusion: ABCD is a square.
     _____

Book 3 • Grade 3

Advanced Concepts

22

Learning to Round Numbers

1. **Round the following numbers to the nearest 10.**

   a. 79 _____   k. 14 _____
   b. 47 _____   l. 86 _____
   c. 31 _____   m. 6 _____
   d. 68 _____   n. 27 _____
   e. 57 _____   o. 11 _____
   f. 49 _____   p. 36 _____
   g. 18 _____   q. 9 _____
   h. 21 _____   r. 16 _____
   i. 66 _____   s. 143 _____
   j. 72 _____   t. 638 _____

2. **Round these numbers to the nearest 100.**

   a. 198 _____   k. 97 _____
   b. 627 _____   l. 504 _____
   c. 484 _____   m. 777 _____
   d. 113 _____   n. 290 _____
   e. 252 _____   o. 90 _____
   f. 811 _____   p. 410 _____
   g. 333 _____   q. 901 _____
   h. 745 _____   r. 638 _____
   i. 401 _____   s. 1,873 _____
   j. 551 _____   t. 2,940 _____

3. **Use the chart to answer the questions.**

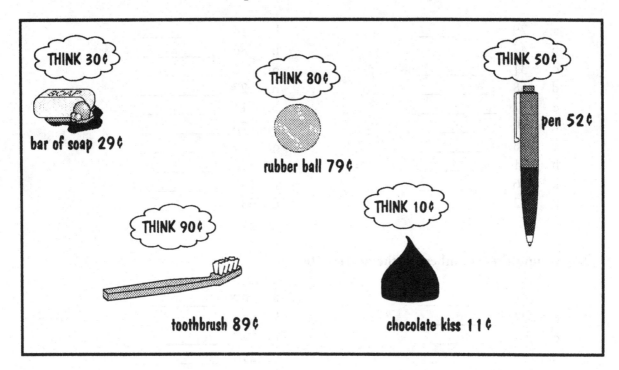

a. Estimate the cost of two toothbrushes. _____

b. Estimate the cost of three bars of soap. _____

c. Estimate the cost of two rubber balls. _____

d. Estimate the cost of four chocolate kisses. _____

e. Estimate the cost of six pens. _____

f Estimate the cost of two bars of soap and two pens. _____

g. Estimate the cost of three chocolate kisses and a toothbrush. _____

h. Estimate the cost of one rubber ball and four pens. _____

i. Estimate the cost of three bars of soap and two toothbrushes. _____

j. About how much would the bill be, if you bought all the items on the chart?
   More or less than $3.00? _____

23 Estimating

1. Estimate the number of apples in the picture.

↑

Count the apples in the first box. Then multiply by 4.
About _____ apples.

2. This pencil is about two inches long:

The side of your desk is about _____ pencils long, so it must be about _____ inches long.

3. Mrs. Adams usually can serve four people with one box of spaghetti. If she wants to cook spaghetti for 18 people, about how many boxes should she use?

About _____ boxes.

4. If one watermelon can feed eight people, about how many watermelons will we need to feed 70 people?

About _____ watermelons.

5. If Mr. Jones sold 123 flags in the morning and 289 in the afternoon on Flag Day, about how many flags did he sell for the day?

Just over _____ flags.

6. Mrs. Connor paid $374 for a lawn mower and $215 for an outdoor grill. Did the bill come to below $600 or above $600?

   Answer: Just _____ $600.

7. Sam lives four miles from Tim. It takes Tim about 30 minutes to ride his bike there. Pete lives two miles beyond Sam. How much time should Tim estimate the bike ride to Pete's house to be?

   About _____ minutes.

8. Rosemary went fishing with her aunt on Saturday. Rosemary caught three mackerel and her aunt caught two. One mackerel usually weighs a little less than four pounds. About how much do you estimate the total weight of their fish to be?

   About _____ lbs.

9. One mackerel can easily feed two people. How many people do you estimate Rosemary and her aunt can invite to dinner on Saturday? (Remember, Rosemary and her aunt will be eating the fish, too.)

   At least _____ people.

10. The city of Lynchburg, VA wants to put in new lights on Main Street. The job will cost about $500,000. The city earns about $5,000 a week in tolls. This money will be used to pay for the work. About how long should Lynchburg estimate it will take to pay for their new lights? (Remember, there are 52 weeks in a year.)

    About _____ years.

24

Finding the Most Reasonable Answer

Directions: Read the facts in the sentences. Then use these facts to choose the best answer from the lists below. Circle the answer. The first one is done for you.

1. John is in the 11th grade. How old is he?
   a. 16 years old   b. 8 years old   c. 21 years old

2. Mr. Farmer collects 80 eggs from his hen house each day. How many hens does he probably have?
   a. 2,000   b. 2   c. 100

3. Pedro can mow the lawn in two hours. His brother, Jose, takes three hours. On Sunday, they work together. About how long should it take them?
   a. 5 hours   b. 4 hours   c. 1½ hours

4. Erica walks to school every day. It takes her about
   a. 20 minutes   b. 3 hours   c. 1½ hours

5. Six roses at the florist cost $2.00. A dozen roses at the same florist costs
   a. $1.00   b. $8.00   c. $4.00

6. Nicole bought her handbag for $30.00. Erica bought the same bag at a 20% sale. Erica paid
   a. $36.00   b. $24.00   c. $80.00

7. Paula runs about two miles a day. In a week she probably runs about
   a. 40 miles   b. 24 miles   c. 12 miles

8. Tracy earns $2.00 a day. In a month she earns
   a. $60.00   b. $80.00   c. $30.00

9. Mona is going to put up a swing in her back yard. She will hang if from a tree branch that is 10 feet above the ground. About how much rope should Mona buy?
   a. 10 feet   b. 20 feet   c. 30 feet

Finding the Most Reasonable Answer (Cont.)

10. George and his father are going to the circus in New Haven, CT. They live 75 miles away. George's father tells him that they will be able to drive about 50 miles per hour all the way to New Haven. The circus starts at 2 p.m. About what time should they leave home?
    a. 11 a.m.   b. 12 p.m.   c. 1 p.m.

11. Kim and his family go to the mountains every summer. One thing they like to do is watch for eagles. In the last five years, they have spotted a total of 25 eagles. About how many of the birds can they expect to see next summer?
    a. 25   b. 5   c. 10

12. It takes Elio 10 minutes to walk to the grocery store. About how far from his home is the store?
    a. eight blocks   b. two blocks   c. one mile

13. A third-grade class of 20 students is making a fish pond. The pond will hold 160 gallons of water. To fill the pond, water must be carried in one-gallon cans from a spring to the new pond. Each student will make the same number of trips from the spring to the pond. They carry a gallon of water each trip. How many trips must each student make?
    a. 80 trips   b. 160 trips   c. 8 trips

14. Traffic is heavy coming across the toll bridge into the city. There are three toll gates on the bridge. At rush hour, about 20 cars are lined up waiting to go through each gate. It takes each car about eight minutes to get through. Then, the city decides to open three more gates. If the amount of cars using the bridge remains the same, what will the waiting time be?
    a. doubled   b. halved   c. about the same

25

Choosing the Correct Operation

A. Directions: Complete the statement by circling the appropriate operation.

		+	-	x	÷
1.	Addition is:	+	-	x	÷
2.	Subtraction is:	+	-	x	÷
3.	Multiplication is:	+	-	x	÷
4.	Division is:	+	-	x	÷
5.	Finding the sum is:	+	-	x	÷
6.	Finding the product is:	+	-	x	÷
7.	Finding the quotient is:	+	-	x	÷
8.	Finding the difference is:	+	-	x	÷
9.	Finding the total is:	+	-	x	÷
10.	Finding more is:	+	-	x	÷
11.	Finding less is:	+	-	x	÷
12.	Three books at two dollars each means:	+	-	x	÷
13.	Twenty dollars for five days means:	+	-	x	÷
14.	Six teams and four teams means:	+	-	x	÷
15.	Eighty games minus 35 games means:	+	-	x	÷
16.	More are needed means:	+	-	x	÷
17.	How many are left means:	+	-	x	÷
18.	The difference between 12 and 16 is:	+	-	x	÷
19.	Twenty-four bottles, six per pack means:	+	-	x	÷
20.	Six cars, four tires per car means:	+	-	x	÷

B. Directions: Read the problem, then complete the sentence with one of these words: add, subtract, multiply, or divide.

21. Terry is taking a trip to visit his grandparents in Chicago, IL. His plane leaves at 4 p.m. His parents drove him to the airport and he arrived at 2:45 p.m. How long does Terry have to wait for his plane?

    To find the answer, I must _____.

22. While he was waiting, Terry decided to buy his grandparents a present. He looked around for a long time. He finally chose a book he thought they would both like. To pay for the book, Terry gave the clerk a $10.00 bill. He received $5.50 in change. How much did the book cost?

    To find the answer, I must _____.

23. Finally, the plane came, and Terry got on board. His plane was a 737. It has 30 rows of seats. There were six seats in each row. Every seat was filled. How many people were flying with Terry?

    To find the answer, I must _____.

24. Six stewardesses were serving snacks on the airplane. They each served the same number of passengers. How many passengers did each stewardess serve?

    To find the answer, I must _____.

25. The captain announced that there were some planes in line ahead of them. For safety reasons, this airport allows four minutes between each plane's takeoff. Their plane will take off in 20 minutes. How many planes are ahead of them?

To find the answer, I must _____.

26. Terry's plane left at 4:20 p.m. The plane ride was 1½ hours long. What time will Terry arrive in Chicago?

To find the answer, I must _____.

Can You Do These Problems?

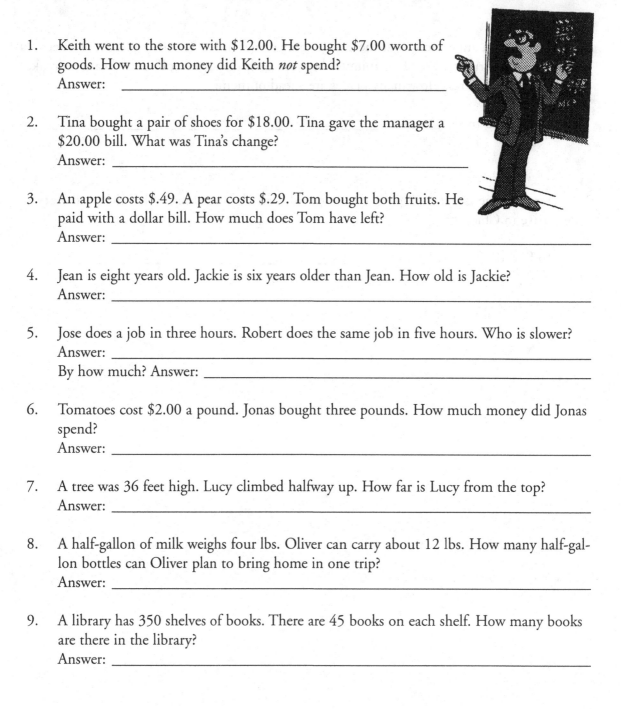

1. Keith went to the store with $12.00. He bought $7.00 worth of goods. How much money did Keith *not* spend?
   Answer: _____

2. Tina bought a pair of shoes for $18.00. Tina gave the manager a $20.00 bill. What was Tina's change?
   Answer: _____

3. An apple costs $.49. A pear costs $.29. Tom bought both fruits. He paid with a dollar bill. How much does Tom have left?
   Answer: _____

4. Jean is eight years old. Jackie is six years older than Jean. How old is Jackie?
   Answer: _____

5. Jose does a job in three hours. Robert does the same job in five hours. Who is slower?
   Answer: _____
   By how much? Answer: _____

6. Tomatoes cost $2.00 a pound. Jonas bought three pounds. How much money did Jonas spend?
   Answer: _____

7. A tree was 36 feet high. Lucy climbed halfway up. How far is Lucy from the top?
   Answer: _____

8. A half-gallon of milk weighs four lbs. Oliver can carry about 12 lbs. How many half-gallon bottles can Oliver plan to bring home in one trip?
   Answer: _____

9. A library has 350 shelves of books. There are 45 books on each shelf. How many books are there in the library?
   Answer: _____

Can You Correct Doug's Homework?

Directions: Read the problems carefully. Correct the ones Doug missed last night.

1. Betty ran three miles on Saturday. She ran five miles on Sunday afternoon. How many more miles did she run on Sunday?
   Doug's Answer: <u>8 miles</u>
   Your Answer: _____

2. Alexi found six tennis balls outside the City Courts. He gave two to his sister, Christina. How many balls did Alexi keep for himself?
   Doug's Answer: <u>4 balls</u>
   Your Answer: _____

3. Mr. Willis bought three shirts for $15.00 each. How much money did Mr. Willis spend?
   Doug's Answer: <u>$35.00</u>
   Your Answer: _____

4. When Ray was five years old, his brother, George, was three years old. Now George is five years old. How old is Ray now?
   Doug's Answer: <u>10 years old</u>
   Your Answer: _____

5. Eighteen pigeons landed on Tony's roof. Tony caught five of them in his net. How many pigeons are now sitting on the roof?
   Doug's Answer: <u>0 pigeons</u>
   Your Answer: _____

6. How many pigeons flew away?
   Doug's Answer: <u>13 pigeons flew away</u>
   Your Answer: _____

7. If for every correct answer you gave Doug five points, how many points did Doug get on last night's homework?
   Your Answer: _____

Counting Figures

1. How many rectangles can you count?

Red	Green
Blue	White

   a. There are _____ one-color rectangles.

   b. There are _____ two-color rectangles.

   c. There is _____ four-color rectangles.

   TOTAL: _____ rectangles in all.

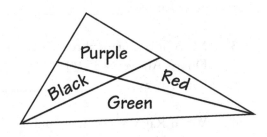

2. How many triangles do you see?

   a. There are _____ one-color triangles.

   b. There are _____ two-color triangles.

   c. There is _____ four-color triangle.

   TOTAL: _____ triangles in all.

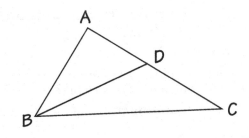

3. How many triangles are there? _____

   Name them. _____

   _____

   _____

4. Can you name five squares?

_____

_____

_____

_____

_____

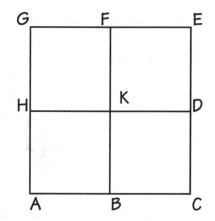

5. Can you name three angles?

Angle _____

Angle _____

Angle _____

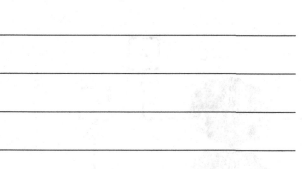

6. How many squares do you see? _____

How many triangles? _____

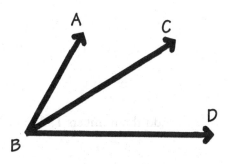

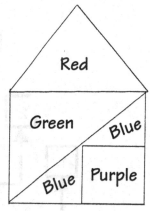

7. How many triangles do you see? _____

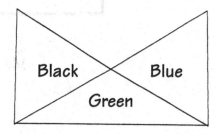

29

Learning To Add Numbers Efficiently

1. Add the numbers 1, 2, 3, 4, 5.

    Example:

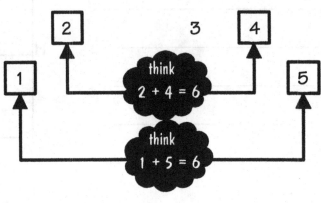

    Add this column: <u>15</u>
    The answer is 15.

2. Add the numbers 1, 2, 3, 4, 5, 6, 7, 8.

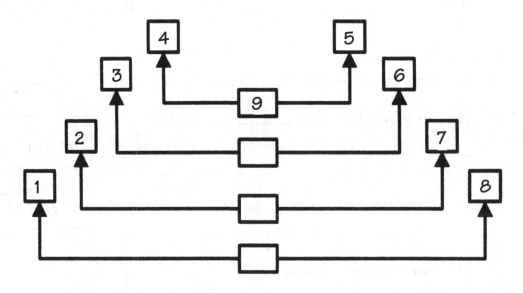

    Add this column: _____

3.   Add the even numbers 2, 4, 6, 8, 10, 12.

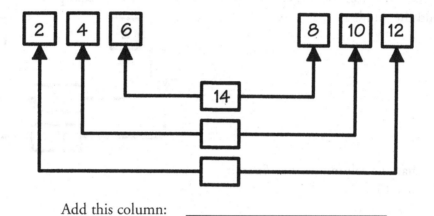

Add this column: _____

4.   Add the odd numbers 1, 3, 5, 7, 9.

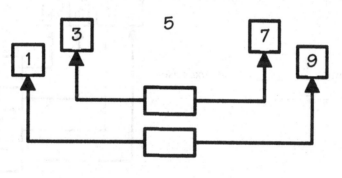

Add this column: _____

5. Add the numbers from 1 through 12.

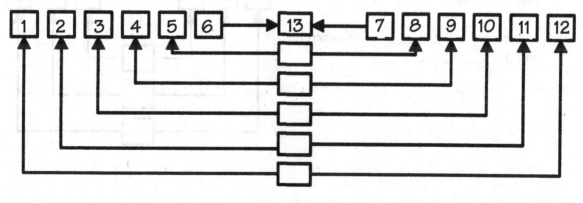

Add this column: _____

30

Becoming An Expert

How can you become an expert in addition?
1. Add the numbers 1, 2, 3, 4.

Example:

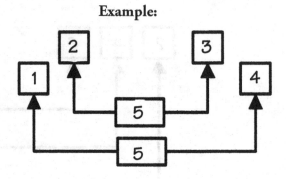

Notice that our column has two 5s in it,
and 2 x 5 = 10.
1 + 2 + 3 + 4 = 10

2. Another example: Add the numbers
    1 through 8.

    There are four _____ in this exercise,
    and 4 x _____ = _____.

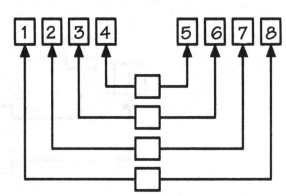

3. Add the numbers 4, 5, 6, 7, 8, 9.

    There are three _____ in this exercise,
    and 3 x _____ = _____.

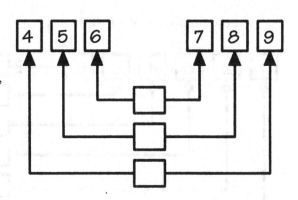

To become an expert in addition, you can change it to multiplication!

Book 4 · Grade 4

Understanding the Problem

31. Finding and Rewriting the Question

Directions: Read the problem carefully. First underline what the problem is asking you to do. Then write the question in your own words. The first one is done for you.

1. A square room with sides of 15 feet is to have a square carpet with sides of 9 feet. <u>How much of the room will stay uncovered?</u>

   The question is: <u>What is the difference between a 15 foot by 15 foot square and a 9 foot by 9 foot square?</u>

2. Maria and Jeff are raking leaves. Both are raking very hard. Each is making a pile of leaves. One of them has been working all morning. The other just started. Maria's pile is larger than Jeff's. Who started raking first?

   The question is: _____

3. If John bought three apples at $.35 each and two oranges at $.15 each, how much did John spend?

   The question is: _____

4. Sam was sent to the nearby store to buy 24 cans of tomato juice. How many six-packs did Sam carry home?

   The question is: _____

5. Linda can finish a job in three hours. Karen can finish the same job in two hours. How long will it take them to finish the job together?

   The question is: _____

32

Underlining and Listing the Facts

Directions: Read the problem carefully. First underline the facts needed to solve the problem. Then write the facts in your own words. The first one is done.

1. Find the perimeter of a rectangular room 24 feet long and 14 feet wide.

   Fact (a): <u>Room is 24 feet long</u>
   Fact (b): <u>Room is 14 feet wide</u>

2. Ellen bought a carpet 9 feet by 9 feet. It is to go in a square room with sides 25 feet. How much of Ellen's floor will stay uncovered?

   Fact (a): _____
   Fact (b): _____

3. How long will it take a bus to travel from Boston to New York if the bus travels at 60 m.p.h., and the distance between the two cities is 240 miles?

   Fact (a): _____
   Fact (b): _____

4. If Henry bought a sandwich for $3.25 and milk for $.75, how much did his lunch cost?

   Fact (a): _____
   Fact (b): _____

5. Sam was sent to the nearby store to buy 24 cans of tomato juice. How many six-packs did Sam carry home?

   Fact (a): _____
   Fact (b): _____

6. Linda can finish a job in three hours. Karen can finish the same job in two hours. How long will it take them to finish the job together?

    Fact (a): _____
    Fact (b): _____

7. Find the area of a rectangular room 10 feet wide and 16 feet long.

    Fact (a): _____
    Fact (b): _____

8. Kate went up five floors, down three, and then up one floor before she found her father's office. How many floors did she travel altogether?

    Fact (a): _____
    Fact (b): _____
    Fact (c): _____

9. There are three ways to go from Tom's house to Dick's house and five ways to go from Dick's to Jane's. How many ways are there from Tom's house to Jane's house?

    Fact (a): _____
    Fact (b): _____

10. If a boat went five miles east, six miles north, and then five miles west, how far is it from its starting position?

    Fact (a): _____
    Fact (b): _____
    Fact (c): _____

33

Using Analogies: Compare and Contrast

Directions: Choose the word that best completes the sentence. Write the word in the blank. The first one is done for you.

1.   Apples are to cider as grapes are to _juice_.

           juice   water   milk   soda

2.   Laughing is to happiness as _____ is to sadness.

           joking   crying   smiling   sleeping

3.   Flock is to birds as _____ is to fish.

           group   family   crowd   school

4.   Snake is to crawling as _____ is to leaping.

           bird   frog   cow   dog

5.   Sugar is to sweet as lemon is to _____.

           yellow   sour   fruit   salt

6.   Clock is to time as _____ is to weight.

         pound   scale   oven   radio

7.   Washington, DC, is to the United States as Paris is to _____.

         England   France   Germany   Mexico

8.   Addition is to subtraction as _____ is to division.

         product   multiplication   sum   quotient

9.   Product is to multiplication as sum is to _____.

         addition   subtraction   multiplication   division

10.   Inch is to foot as ounce is to _____.

         weight   kilo   gram   pound

11.   Problem is to solution as _____ is to answer.

         number   exercise   experiment   question

12. Seven is to 49 as _____ is to 81.

    11   9   8   6

13. 5/5 is to 1.0 as _____ is to 1.0.

    7.0   1.0   7/7   .7

14. 1/2 is to .5 as 1/4 is to _____.

    .25   4.0   3/4   .20

15. is to 1/3 as is to _____.

    1/5   3   1/4   4

16. is to 3/4 as is to _____.

    1/3   1/2   1/4   .25

17. is to 2/5 as is to _____.

    4/5   1/3   1/2   4/6

34

Putting Events in Order

Directions: Read each paragraph carefully. Then rewrite it in the order the events happened.

1. Paula ran to school. Paula jumped out of bed. The bell rang just as she got to the classroom. She dressed and ate breakfast in 10 minutes.

   _____
   _____
   _____
   _____
   _____
   _____

2. The Indians waited for the sun and rain to ripen the corn. On top of the fish they sowed the corn. They placed a dead fish in it. The Indians dug a shallow hole. They covered the hole with soil.

   _____
   _____
   _____
   _____
   _____
   _____

3. The honeybee makes a beeline for home. The honeybee finds the flowers by following their sweet smell. Back at the hive, she dances to tell the others where the food is. The honeybee collects the nectar and pollen.

   _____
   _____
   _____
   _____
   _____
   _____

Putting Events in Order *(Cont.)*

4. Cut the fabric following the directions of the pattern. Sew the dress. Select a pattern for the dress. Buy the fabric and the thread that you need.

_____
_____
_____
_____
_____
_____

5. Measure window. Buy new glass. Break window. Install window. Remove broken glass.

_____
_____
_____
_____
_____
_____

6. Open your mouth and speak. Listen to what your teacher is asking. Think! Raise your hand.

_____
_____
_____
_____
_____
_____

A. Directions: One sentence in the following paragraph is not necessary to answer the question. Find this sentence and draw a line through it.

Every year, rabbits eat some of the vegetables in our garden. They eat the carrots and the lettuce. We do not grow flowers in our garden. The rabbits do not eat the tomatoes. They do not seem to bother the squash.
Question: Which vegetables do the rabbits enjoy?

B. Directions: Underline the two phrases that show what Melinda must do. Draw a line through the phrase that is not important.

Melinda is planning to make a dinner dessert for her parents tonight. She must:
decide on a recipe.
send away for a cookbook.
buy the ingredients needed.

C. Directions: Read the following problems carefully. Cross out the fact or facts that are not needed. Then solve the problem.

1. John gathered three bushels of apples in one hour.
   Paul gathered five bushels of apples in two hours.
   How many bushels did they gather altogether? _____

2. The furniture company has 30 couches in stock. They sold eight couches Friday evening and 14 couches on Saturday. How many couches did they sell for the two days? _____

3. Mr. Book bought 17 cows at $200 each and 12 cows at $300 each. How many cows did he buy altogether? _____

4.   The Red Sox played 12 games in the last two weeks. They won four of them. How many did they lose? _____

5.   Jean jogged three miles in 20 minutes for warmup. Then she ran two more miles in a race in 12 minutes flat. How long did she exercise for the day?_____
_____

6.   John read three books during his summer vacation. Tom read five, and Judy read six. How many books did the boys read? _____

7.   A baseball bat costs $9.00, and a baseball costs $4.00.
How much do seven baseballs cost? _____

8.   Mrs. Jones went to the supermarket. She bought three pounds of fresh beans, five cans of tuna fish, three cans of frozen orange juice, and two cans of baked beans. The total bill was $22.57. How many cans did she bring home? _____

9.   Bill and Allen went duck hunting. Allen got three Black Ducks, two Red Hooded Mergansers, and one male Bufflehead. Bill got one Black Duck and two Canadian geese. If the limit was 10 birds per person, per day, how many did Bill need to reach his limit? _____

10.   George had a great day against the Mustangs. He had 18 strikeouts, two walks, and held the Mustangs scoreless through six innings. His team finally won four to one in nine innings. How many Mustangs did George strike out, on average per inning? _____
_____

36

Adding the Missing Fact

Directions: One more fact is needed to answer the questions in the following problems. Check the necessary fact. The first one is done.

1. Alex left for the library at 11 a.m. What time did she get there?

    _____ (a) The library was 200 yards away.
    _✓_ (b) It took her 10 minutes to walk.
    _____ (c) The library opens at 11:15.

2. Leo has saved $42.00. How much does he need to buy a bike?

    _____ (a) He wants to buy a three-speed bike.
    _____ (b) The bike costs $65.00.
    _____ (c) The store closes at 8 p.m.

3. Mrs. Miller is the cook at Sweetwater Summer Camp. She needs to know how many dozen eggs to order for Tuesday's breakfast of bacon and eggs. She plans to serve two eggs per person.

    _____ (a) The summer camp is located in the Catskills.
    _____ (b) There are two canoes and one rowboat for the campers.
    _____ (c) This week, there are 24 campers at Sweetwater.

4. Richard and Tom are brothers. Their dad gives them an allowance each week. Richard, who is the older, receives $2.00 per week. How much does Tom have after six weeks?

    _____ (a) Richard has $9.00 at the end of six weeks.
    _____ (b) Tom's allowance is $1.50 a week.
    _____ (c) Dad comes home at 7 p.m.

5. Betty has $30.00. How much money does she have left after buying a soccer ball?

    _____ (a) The store has eight soccer balls.
    _____ (b) Baseballs cost $4.50 each.
    _____ (c) The price of a soccer ball is $27.95.

6. Charles has a 45-minute train ride. What time did he get home?

    _____ (a) School was out at 3:15.
    _____ (b) He got on the train at 3:30.
    _____ (c) He takes the train five days a week.

7. Mrs. Jones came home with Linda and Jo only to find that her favorite raspberry pie had been eaten. Her younger daughter, Rebecca, was playing with their dog, Brittany. Who ate the pie?

    _____ (a) Mrs. Jones came home at 8 p.m.
    _____ (b) Jo was hungry.
    _____ (c) Rebecca was allergic to berries.

8. Matt, Adam, and Joshua are wearing sneakers. Two of the boys are wearing red sneakers, and one is wearing white sneakers. Matt is wearing red sneakers. What color sneakers is Adam wearing?

    _____ (a) Matt and Adam are brothers.
    _____ (b) Joshua's sneakers are white.
    _____ (c) Adam is wearing high-top sneakers.

9. Jose, Pedro, and Ann each own a bike: a three-speed, a 10-speed, and a dirt bike. Jose does not own a 10-speed. What kind of bike does Ann have?

    _____ (a) Jose lent his bike to Ann.
    _____ (b) Jose likes to ride fast.
    _____ (c) Pedro has a dirt bike.

Using Facts to Draw Conclusions

Directions: Fill in the blanks to complete these sentences.

1. If 12 ⬭ make a dozen, then _____ ⬭ must make a half dozen.

2. If a month has four weeks, then three months must have _____ weeks.

3. If there are 24 hours in a day, then six hours make _____ of a day.

4. If each omelet takes two eggs, then two dozen eggs will make _____ omelets.

5. If there are six cars, and each car has four wheels, then we need_____ tires for all the cars.

6. If all ▲s have three sides, which of these figures are ▲s? _____

    a. ◇   b. ⋀   c. ◺   d. ⬠   e. ◁

7. If there are 36 bottles and four boxes, then we must have _____ bottles in each box.

8. If there are four cages, and each cage contains two animals, and each animal has four legs, then there must be _____ legs.

9. If a car takes eight gallons of gasoline to go 72 miles, then it must get _____ miles per gallon.

10. If a whole pizza was divided equally among three people, then each person got_____ pieces.

Using Facts to Answer Questions

Directions: Underline the facts you will need to answer these questions. Write the answer on the lines.

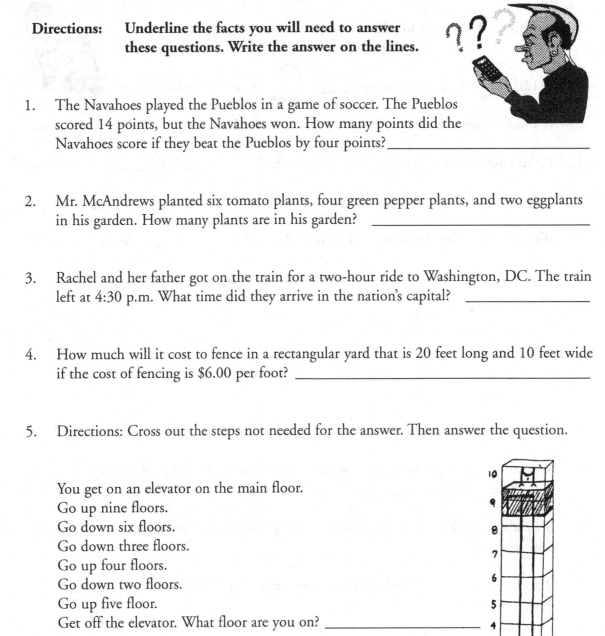

1. The Navahoes played the Pueblos in a game of soccer. The Pueblos scored 14 points, but the Navahoes won. How many points did the Navahoes score if they beat the Pueblos by four points? _____

2. Mr. McAndrews planted six tomato plants, four green pepper plants, and two eggplants in his garden. How many plants are in his garden? _____

3. Rachel and her father got on the train for a two-hour ride to Washington, DC. The train left at 4:30 p.m. What time did they arrive in the nation's capital? _____

4. How much will it cost to fence in a rectangular yard that is 20 feet long and 10 feet wide if the cost of fencing is $6.00 per foot? _____

5. Directions: Cross out the steps not needed for the answer. Then answer the question.

   You get on an elevator on the main floor.
   Go up nine floors.
   Go down six floors.
   Go down three floors.
   Go up four floors.
   Go down two floors.
   Go up five floor.
   Get off the elevator. What floor are you on? _____

Using Facts to Solve Problems

A. Five fourth-grade boys always check with one another to decide what color jacket they will wear to school the next day. Each of the boys has two jackets.

Joey has a blue jacket and a green jacket.
Bert has a red jacket and an orange jacket.
Carlo has a purple jacket and a white jacket.
Andre has a blue jacket and a yellow jacket.
Kirum has a brown jacket and a purple jacket.

They agreed on what color jacket each would wear. Read each fact and answer the questions to decide what color jacket each boy will wear to school tomorrow. Color each boy's jacket correctly.

FACTS:

- No two boys will wear the same color jacket.
- Joey, Bert, and Carlo's jackets will represent the colors of the American Flag.
- Kirum will not wear his purple jacket unless Carlo wears his purple jacket.

QUESTIONS:

1.	Will Joey wear his blue jacket?	❑ yes	❑ no
2.	Will Andre wear his blue jacket?	❑ yes	❑ no
3.	Will Bert wear his orange jacket?	❑ yes	❑ no
4.	Will Kirum wear his brown jacket?	❑ yes	❑ no
5.	Will Carlo wear his white jacket?	❑ yes	❑ no

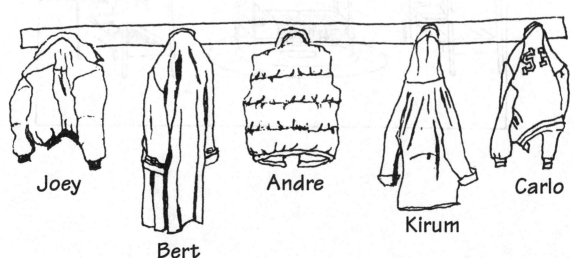

Joey   Bert   Andre   Kirum   Carlo

B. Directions: Read Roger's letter and decide who sleeps in each bunk. Then write the name on the correct bed.

Dear Mom and Dad,

I am having a great time at camp. We go swimming and hiking. There are six boys in my cabin. The other kids' names are Tom, Joe, Max, Dan, and Pete. We sleep in bunk beds. Tom and I share a bunk bed. Joe and Max share a bunk bed. Dan sleeps on the lower bunk next to the window. Max sleeps between Tom and Dan. I sleep above Tom. We are all good friends.

Your son,
Roger

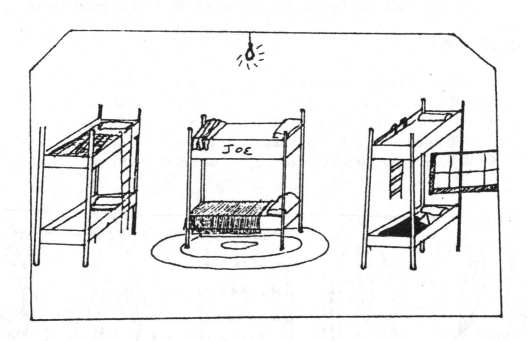

40

Using Facts and Questions to Solve Problems

Directions: Read all the facts. Then answer the questions to help you solve the problem.

Four zoo animals are to be taken to another zoo in two cages.
The animals are Margo, Bert, Chico, and Daisy.

- Margo always fights with Daisy.
- Bert eats all of Margo's food.
- Chico gets along with all zoo creatures.

Questions:

a. Would you place Margo and Daisy in the same cage?
    ❏ yes   ❏ no

b. Would you place Bert and Margo in the same cage?
    ❏ yes   ❏ no

c. Would you place Chico and Margo in the same cage?
    ❏ yes   ❏ no

Using the facts and your answers, write the names of the animals in the two cages.

_____	_____
_____	_____

CAGE 1   CAGE 2

1. Directions: Use the following model to help you prove your answer.

We can see that birds have feathers. The feathers of many birds are very colorful. The toucan is an example of a colorful bird. The crow, however, is a bird that is completely black.

Question: Does a crow have feathers? _____

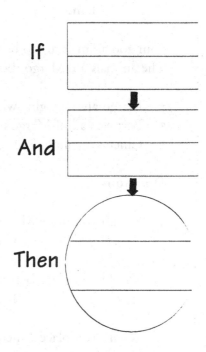

    a. Find the main fact of the paragraph and write it in the IF box.

    b. Locate a fact related to the main fact and write it in the AND box.

    c. Use the information from the main fact IF and second fact AND to write a final fact.

    d. Decide whether THEN is True or False.

       T   F

2.   A book is made up of pages. Each page contains words and information. Each page of a dictionary lists words and their meanings. Dictionaries are found in schools, libraries, and most homes. Dictionaries are important to everyone. Question: Is the dictionary a book?

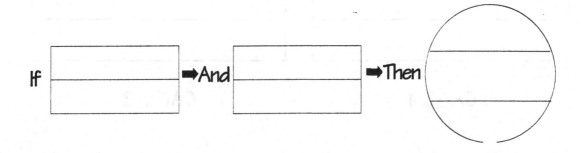

Book 5 · Grade 4

Using Charts, Graphs, Diagrams, and Other Illustrations

42

Solving Problems Using Tables & Graphs

A. Directions: Use this table to answer the questions below.

	Atlanta	Boston	Cleveland	Detroit	Houston	Los Angeles	Miami	New York
Atlanta		937	554	596	701	1936	604	748
Boston	937		551	613	1605	2596	1255	188
Cleveland	554	551		90	*	2049	1087	405
Detroit	596	613	90		1105	1983	1152	482
Houston	701	1605	1114	1105		1374	968	1420
Los Angeles	1936	2596	2049	1983	1374		2339	2451
Miami	604	1255	?	1152	968	2339		1092
New York	748	188	405	482	1420	2451	1092	

Air miles between major cities

1. The ? in the table means the distance between which cities? _____

2. How many air miles is it from Houston to Los Angeles? _____

3. Which is farthest from Los Angeles—Miami, New York, or Boston? _____

4. Which is the closest city to Houston on this table? _____

5. The air distance from Cleveland to New York is _____.

6. I have a ticket out of New York good for 1,000 miles. To how many cities can I travel?
   _____

7. If an airplane flies at 500 miles per hour, about how long will it take to go from Atlanta to Los Angeles? _____

8. What number goes in the * space? _____

Solving Problems Using Tables & Graphs *(Cont.)*

B. Directions: This graph shows the cost of ribbon in feet. For example, to find the cost of six feet of ribbon, go up the six feet line, meet the graph, and look left along the horizontal line to read $1.80. Use the graph to answer the questions.

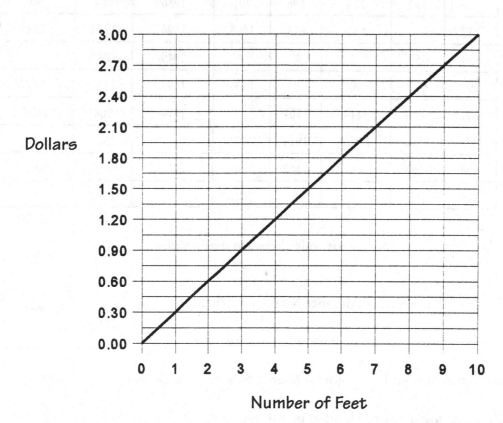

1. What is the cost of four feet of ribbon? _____
2. How much would you pay for two yards? _____
3. If Paula spent $2.10, how many feet did she buy? _____
4. At this rate, how much would three yards cost? _____
5. What is the cost of 2/3 of a yard? _____
6. How long a ribbon will you buy for $3.00? _____
7. How much would 18 inches of ribbon cost? _____

43

Solving Problems Using Charts

Directions: Study the pie chart below. Use the facts to answer each question on the opposite page.

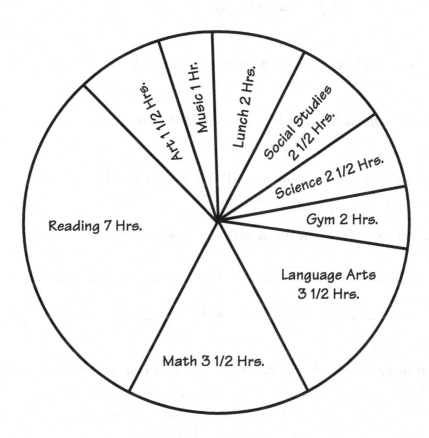

School Week Activity Chart

1. In what subject area is the most time spent? _____

2. In what subject area is the least time spent? _____

3. How many hours per week are spent on Math and Science together? _____

4. How long is the student's work week, not including lunch? _____

5. How much more time is spent in Math class than in Lunch? _____

6. Name two pairs of subjects that receive equal time:

    a. _____ and   b. _____

    c. _____ and   d. _____

7. Do Language Arts, Math, and Reading account for more or less than half the time in school? _____

8. Is the time spent for Reading more, less, or equal to 1/4 of the time the student spends in school? _____

9. By how many times does Reading exceed Math time? _____

10. According to the chart, how much time do the students spend in Economics class? ____

    _____

44

Solving Problems Using Illustrations

A. Directions: Dan was planning a parade. There were four zoo animals to lead the parade. There was a monkey, a tiger, a zebra, and an elephant. Dan knew that:

- the tiger didn't get along with the monkey.

- the monkey would hold the zebra's tail.

- the elephant would lead the parade.

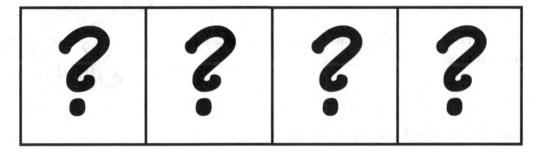

Answer the questions to help you solve the problem.

1. Which animal is first? _____

2. What animal would not be next to the tiger? _____

3. What animal would be in front of the monkey? _____

4. What animal would come after the elephant? _____

5. Write the name of each animal in the correct box.

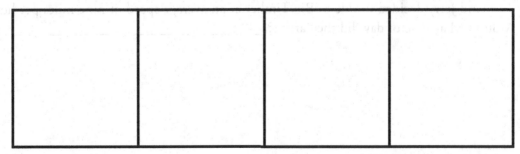

Solving Problems Using Illustrations *(Cont.)*

B. Directions Tom and Jerry arrived at this sign at noon
Wednesday on their bicycling trip.

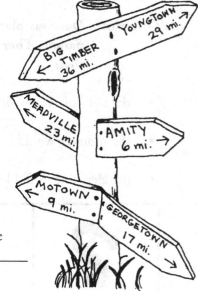

1. Which is the farthest town that Tom and Jerry could bike
    to from here? _____

2. How far is it from Meadville to Georgetown? _____

3. If Tom and Jerry could bike around 10 miles per hour, about how long will it take them
    to go to Youngtown? _____

4. How many miles will they travel if Tom and Jerry decided to go to Motown first and then
    to Amity? _____

5. Tom and Jerry decided to ride to Big Timber at an average speed of nine miles per hour.
    Around what time of day did they arrive? _____

45

Solving Problems Using Illustrations

1. Sheila sees three triangles in the following diagram. Can you help her name them? One of them is

    a. _____ABD_____
    b. _____
    c. _____

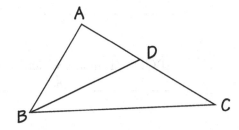

2. Can you name the five squares?

    a. _____
    b. _____
    c. _____
    d. _____
    e. _____

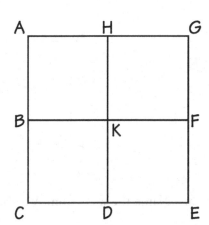

3. How many squares and how many triangles can you see? How many rectangles are there?

    a) _____ squares
    b) _____ triangles
    c) _____ rectangles

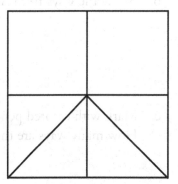

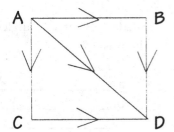

4. a. How many ways are there to go from A to D if
        the streets are one-way as shown?
        _____ ways

    b. If ABCD is a square, which two routes are equal?
        _____ and _____

    c. Which is the shortest route from A to C?_____

5.

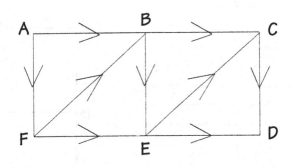

    a. Name the ways from A to B. _____
        _____

    b. Name the ways from A to E. _____
        _____
        _____

    c. Mark with colored pencil the ways to go from A to C.
        How many ways are there? _____

    d. Count the ways from A to D. _____

46

Using Facts To Solve Riddles

Riddle: **Who will be Mr. Edgar's future wife?**

Directions: **Use the map on the opposite page to answer these questions. Then match the letters in your answers with the numbers of the blanks in the Answer Key. You will find out the name of Mr. Edgar's future wife.**

1.   How far is it from Boston to Westwood? _____ (M)

2.   How many towns are the same distance away from Boston? _____ (A)

3.   How many towns are at least 10 miles away from Boston? _____ (S)

4.   How many miles will you put on a car if you go from Braintree to Boston and back? _____(D)

5.   How many towns are there west of Boston?_____ (R)

6.   How much farther is Cohasset from Boston than Natick? _____ (G)

7.   How many towns are within 15 miles of Boston? _____ (R)

8.   How far is the farthest town from Boston on this map? _____ (E)

Answer Key

___	___	___	___	___	___	___	___
10	7	9	45	24	13	2	6

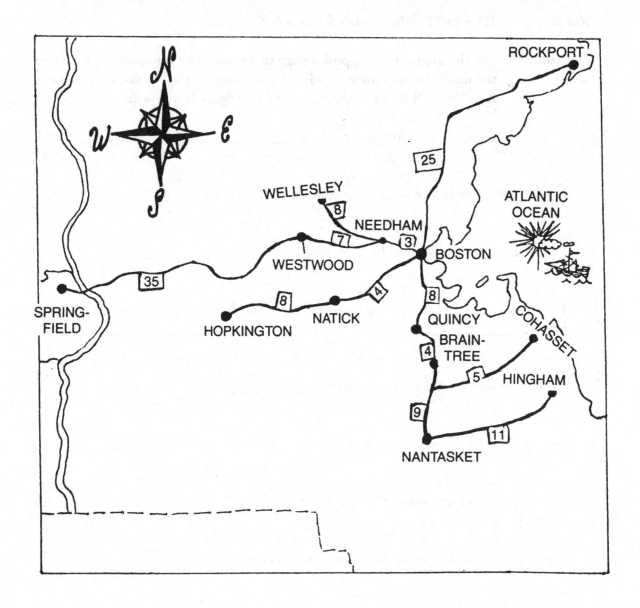

A Riddle Problem

Riddle: ***What is it you cannot see yet is always before you?***

Directions: **Use the map on the opposite page to answer these questions. Then match the letters in your answers with the numbers beneath the blanks in the Answer Key. Write the letters in the blanks to solve the riddle.**

1.   How far is it from Kennedy to Adams? _____ (T)

2.   How many cities are south of Kennedy? _____ (U)

3.   How many cities are less than eight miles from Kennedy? _____ (F)

4.   How many letters does the name of the farthest city from Kennedy have? _____ (H)

5.   What is the total mileage from Mickey to Reagan and back? _____ (R)

6.   How many cities on this map have names belonging to U.S. Presidents? _____ (E)

Answer Key

___   ___   ___   ___   ___   ___   ___   ___   ___
12   5   7   4   3   12   3   16   7

A Riddle Problem *(Cont.)*

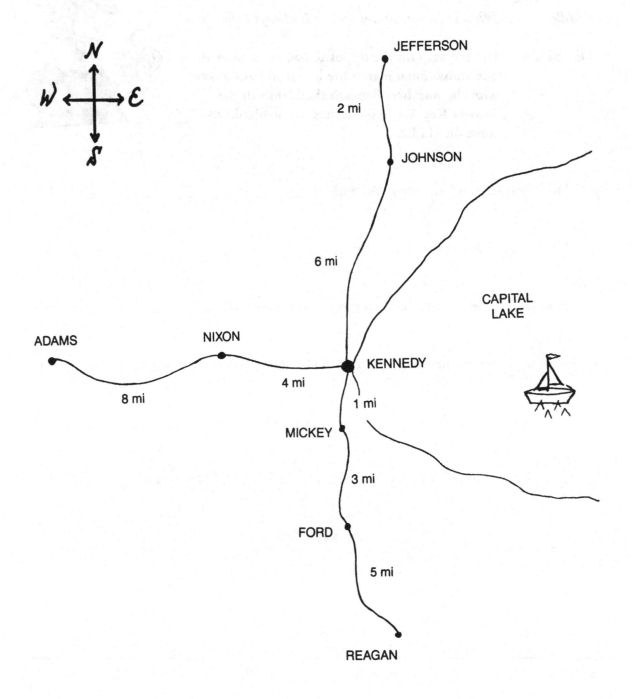

48

Making a Table to Solve a Problem

Directions: Fill in the table below to solve this problem.

Donald collects nickels, dimes, and quarters. He has the following coins:

1984 dime	1987 dime
1987 quarter	1984 nickel
1985 nickel	1985 dime
1984 quarter	1986 quarter
1986 dime	1985 quarter

If Donald wants to complete his coin collection for the years 1984–1987, which coins does he need?

COINS

YEARS	Nickels	Dimes	Quarters
1984			
1985			
1986			
1987			

Book G • Grade 4

Advanced Problem Solving Strategies

49

Looking for Patterns

Directions: Look for a pattern. Then write the last three numbers in these charts.

1.

7	14	21	28	35			

2.

64	49	36	25	16			

3.

1/2	2/3	3/4	4/5	5/6			

4.

1/2	1	3/2	2	5/2			

5.

1/4	1/2	3/4	1	5/4			

Looking for Patterns

Directions: Study the diagrams. Look for a pattern. What numbers belong in the circles? Write them.

1. 2
    3
    5
    6
    11
    4
    ◯ (HINT: Think "+")

2. 2
    3
    6
    3
    ◯
    18
    36 (HINT: Think "x")

3. 36
    12
    3
    4
    2
    ◯
    ◯
    (HINT: Think "factoring")

4.

1	2	3	4
	➡		5
⬆	◯		⬇
		⬅	

Looking for Patterns *(Cont.)*

5.

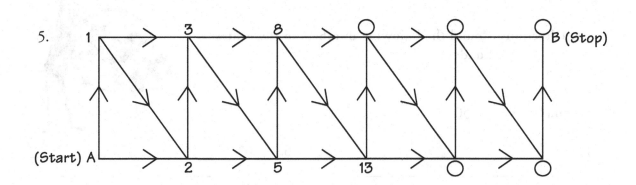

6.

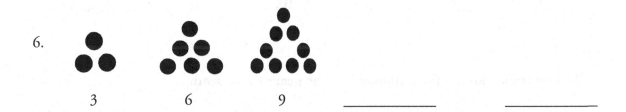

| 3 | 6 | 9 | _____ | _____ |

7. _____ _____ 11 8 5 8 11 _____ _____

Rounding Numbers

A. Directions: Round the following numbers to the nearest hundred.

Example: 483 → <u>500</u>

1.	305 _____	6.	163 _____
2.	789 _____	7.	425 _____
3.	114 _____	8.	590 _____
4.	277 _____	9.	532 _____
5.	350 _____	10.	666 _____

B. Directions: Round these numbers to the nearest thousand.

1.	4876 _____	6.	2855 _____
2.	999 _____	7.	4628 _____
3.	5543 _____	8.	2100 _____
4.	1234 _____	9.	3333 _____
5.	8799 _____	10.	8511 _____

C. Directions: Round these prices to the nearest dollar.

Example: $2.89 → <u>$3.00</u>

1.	$2.25 _____	6.	$2.89 _____
2.	$9.99 _____	7.	$ .75 _____
3.	$6.50 _____	8.	$3.13 _____
4.	$9.29 _____	9.	$1.19 _____
5.	$ .84 _____	10.	$6.66 _____

Solving Problems By Estimating

Directions: In the following problems, first round each number in your head. Then add the rounded numbers to estimate the answer.

1. Mary went to the grocery store. She bought a yogurt for $.79, a box of cereal for $2.29, and milk for $1.65. Estimate about how much Mary spent. About $ _____

2. The park department wanted to know about how many children took summer swimming lessons in the town. At Oyster Pond, 214 children were enrolled; 127 at Sunset Lake; and 83 at Lovers Lake. About how many children took swimming lessons in the town? About _____children

3.

Long's Drug Store Price List			
Toothbrush $.79	Soap $.29	Barrette $.21	Band-Aids $.89

   a. Erica had $2.00 to spend. Could she buy a toothbrush, Band-Aids, and a barrette? _____

   b. Nicole bought all four items. About how much did she spend?
   About _____

   c. About how much would four bars of soap cost?
   About _____

   d. About how much would three toothbrushes cost?
   About _____

Estimating The Most Reasonable Answer

Directions: Check the most reasonable answer to each problem.

1. Mr. Miller went to the supermarket and bought a jar of peanut butter for $1.99; three loaves of bread for $.89 each, a watermelon for $5.99, and two pounds of tomatoes at $1.49 a pound. Mr. Miller's bill should be:

   _____ over $20.00
   _____ around $15.00
   _____ below $10.00
   _____ around $50.00

2. A car goes 15 miles on one gallon of gasoline. Its tank can hold 20 gallons of gasoline. How many miles would you expect to travel on a full tank of gasoline?

   _____ probably around 35 miles
   _____ around 30 miles
   _____ about 600 miles
   _____ 300 miles is a reasonable distance

3. Mrs. Miller is the cook at Sweetwater Summer Camp. She needs to know about how many dozen eggs to order for Tuesday's breakfast of bacon and eggs. This week there are 40 campers and 12 counselors at the camp. She plans to serve two eggs to each person. She will need about

   _____ 60 dozen eggs
   _____ two dozen eggs
   _____ 10 dozen eggs
   _____ 100 dozen eggs

4. One out of every three rivers is polluted in Norfolk County. Norfolk County has about 100 rivers. How many rivers would you expect to find polluted in Norfolk County?

_____ all 100 rivers

_____ around three rivers

_____ approximately 67 rivers

_____ about 33 rivers

5. Tom gets a haircut every six weeks. About how many haircuts will Tom get in a year? (Remember, a year has 52 weeks.)

_____ 46 haircuts

_____ nine haircuts

_____ eight haircuts

_____ 58 haircuts

6. Carol likes to play tennis and read books during her summer vacation. Last summer, she read about two books a week. About how many books were on Carol's summer reading list?

_____ 120 books

_____ 50 books

_____ 24 books

_____ six books

Making Comparisons

Directions: The key idea in these problems is to estimate the cost per unit and then make a comparison.

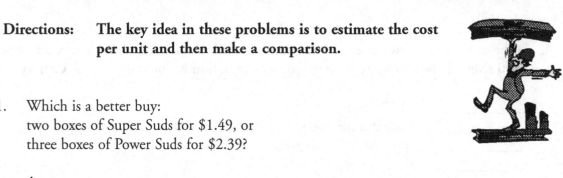

1. Which is a better buy:
   two boxes of Super Suds for $1.49, or
   three boxes of Power Suds for $2.39?

   Answer:
   Cost per box of Super Suds is about _____.
   Cost per box of Power Suds is about _____.
   So, _____ is the better buy. It is cheaper per box.

2. Which is a better paying job:
   $100 for five days, or
   $3.00 on Monday, $6.00 on Tuesday, $12.00 on Wednesday,
        $24.00 on Thursday, $48.00 on Friday?

   Answer: _____

3. Which is less expensive:
   one pound of white cheese at $3.79, or
   two pounds of yellow cheese at $6.49?

   Answer: _____

4. John finished a puzzle working 2½ hours each day for three days. Linda finished the same
   puzzle in eight hours. Who finished the puzzle in a shorter amount of time?

   Answer: _____

Making Comparisons *(Cont.)*

5. Which will give you more money:
   three pennies doubling every day for a week or
   one penny doubling every day for two weeks?

   Answer: _____

6. Mr. Jones sold 100 hamburgers from 9 a.m. to 5 p.m. on Tuesday. Mr. Burger sold 12 hamburgers per hour for eight hours on the same day. Who sold more hamburgers on Tuesday?

   Answer: _____

7. Which costs more:
   red ribbon at $.79 a yard or
   green ribbon at $.16 a foot?

   Answer: _____

8. Alexi got the shaded part.
   Leo got the clear part.
   Who got the bigger piece?

   Answer: _____

9. Leo ate the shaded part this time. Alexi ate the clear part. Who ate the smaller piece?

   Answer: _____

10. ABC is

    _____ a shorter distance
    _____ a longer distance
    _____ the same distance as ADC?

Problems with Multiple Solutions

Directions: The following problems have more than one answer. Find at least three for each.

1. Tina would like to spend her $.36 on the following items. What can she buy if she spends all of it?

| 12¢ | 24¢ | 15¢ | 10¢ | 6¢ |

Answer: Tina can buy

a. _____ squares. Or

b. one _____ and one _____ Or

c. _____ parallelograms and _____ circle.

Can you write two other solutions of your own? (What else can she buy?)

d) _Two triangles and one circle._ _____

e) _____

f) _____

2. Annie has $1.00 in her pocket made up of nickels, dimes, quarters, and half dollars. If she has six coins in all, what could they be?

Hint: Complete the following table.

	.50	.25	.10	.05	Total
answer (a)					$1.00
answer (b)		███		███	$1.00
answer (c)	███				$1.00

A Dart Board Problem

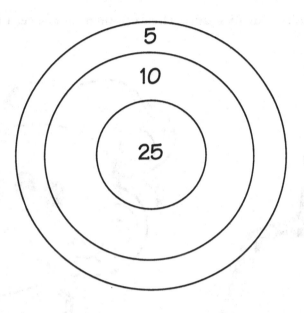

(The second question is done for you.)

1. What is the least number of darts you will use to score 100 points?

    _____

2. How can you score 60 points using four darts?
    _____2 in 25 points_____ and _____2 in 5 points_____

3. How can you score 60 points using three darts?
    _____ and _____

4. How can you score a 50 by using six darts?
    _____ and _____
    or _____ and _____

5. John was able to score a 50 with seven darts. How did he do it?
    _____ and _____

Directions: Look at the diagrams. Then use them to answer the questions.

Speed of Light =
About 186,000 miles
per second

Speed of Sound =
About 750 miles
per hour

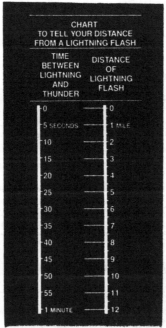

CHART
TO TELL YOUR DISTANCE
FROM A LIGHTNING FLASH

TIME BETWEEN LIGHTNING AND THUNDER	DISTANCE OF LIGHTNING FLASH
0	0
5 SECONDS	1 MILE
10	2
15	3
20	4
25	5
30	6
35	7
40	8
45	9
50	10
55	11
1 MINUTE	12

Using Facts to Draw Conclusions *(Cont.)*

Have you ever been in your home during a thunderstorm and seen lightning in the distance? Did you wonder how far away the lightning was? Did you hear thunder? The thunder and lightning are happening at the same time. You can tell your distance from a lightning flash because of the difference between the speed of light and the speed of sound.

1. Which is faster, the speed of light or the speed of sound? _____

2. Which travels faster, thunder or lightning? _____

3. Remember! The thunder and lightning are happening at the same time. Would you see the lightning first or would you hear the thunder?_____

You can count the seconds between the flash you see and the thunder you hear. Then, using the table on page 12, find how far away the lightning is.

4. You see the lightning. After five seconds, you hear the roll of thunder. How far away is the lightning? _____

5. You see lightning again. After 15 seconds, you hear the thunder crack. How far away is the lightning? _____

6. Again you see a flash of lightning. After 25 seconds, you hear the roll of thunder. How far away is the lightning? _____

7. Is the storm coming closer to your home or going further away? _____

A Good Way to Add Numbers

Directions: Add the numbers given below. Try to group them so that your addition will become easier and quicker. Use a separate piece of paper to do the figuring.

1. Example: 5 + 12 + 3 + 8 + 15

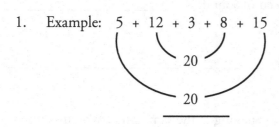

20

20

———

43

2.   1 + 4 + 7 + 10 + 13 = _____

3.   1 + 11 + 21 + 31 + 41 = _____

4.   7 + 6 + 5 + 4 + 3 = _____

5.   14 + 9 + 15 + 21 + 16 + 15 = _____

6.   17 + 2 + 14 + 11 + 8 + 23 + 25 = _____

7.   47 + 62 + 33 + 13 + 8 + 17 = _____

8.   1 + 2 + 3 + 4 + 5 + 6 + 7 + 8 + 9 = _____

9.   4 + 8 + 6 + 11 + 12 + 1 + 6 = _____

10.   55 + 50 + 65 + 45 + 75 + 35 = _____

End of the Year Party!

Directions: Read the paragraph below. Then use your problem solving skills to answer the questions.

Nina was asked to plan a party for her class at the end of the school year. Each student gave her $3.00, so she had $72.00 to spend on the party. She planned that each student would have two pieces of pizza and a can of juice at the party. She ordered eight pizzas at $7.00 each and a case of juice for $8.00. Nina spent the rest of the money on dessert. At the bakery, she bought one cupcake for each of her classmates.

1. How many students are in Nina's class? _____

2. How many pieces of pizza will Nina need for her class? _____

3. To have the correct number of slices, should Nina have pizzas divided into eight or six equal pieces? _____

4. How much did Nina spend on the pizza and juice? _____

5. How much money does Nina have left to spend on dessert? _____

6. If she spent all of this money, about how much did each cupcake cost?
   About_____

Can You Solve These Problems?

1. John bought:
   three apples at $.25 each
   two oranges at $.15 each
   How much did John spend? _____

2. Leo bought:
   24 cans of juice
   The cans were in six-packs.
   How many six-packs did Leo carry home? _____ six-packs

3. The distance from Boston to New York is 240 miles.
   The bus travels at 60 m.p.h.
   How long will the bus trip take? _____ hours

4. The playground is rectangular
   The longer side is 85 feet.
   The shorter side is 43 feet.
   The cost of the fence is $6.00 per foot.
   How much will it cost to fence the playground? _____

5. The Giants were six points ahead of the Patriots at half-time. If the Giants had 14 points, what was the Patriots' point total at half-time? _____ points

6. John counted his baseball cards. Here is his list:

Year	Number of cards
1985	237
1986	475
1987	709
1988	590

About how many baseball cards does John own? About _____cards

Book 7 · Grade 5

Problem Solving Subskills

61

Using Facts to Solve Problems

Supporting Information: Your class is taking a field trip to the Seaside Aquarium. The time to be spent there is one and one-half hours, or 90 minutes. The trip is in connection with the unit you are studying on ocean life. The unit will focus on shellfish and aquatic mammals such as whales, seals, and porpoises. Each session at the aquarium is one-half hour. Read the ad from the Seaside Aquarium. Which sessions will best help you to complete the unit?

Seaside Aquarium

The Seaside Aquarium is as close to being in the ocean as you can get! The 10 huge tanks hold animals that range in size from the tiny minnow to the elephant seal. We have over 50 species of fish, including the jelly fish, the electric eel, and the white shark. You may choose among the following sessions:

A: A guided tour of the 10 tanks;

B: A guided tour of the two-story machine plant that pumps, circulates, and changes the salt water 24 hours a day;

C: A 30-minute color movie entitled "Dolphins, Sharks, and Whales";

D: A slide presentation about how the Aquarium is financed; or

E: A lecture and tour of a separate tank that holds only crabs, shrimp, lobsters, clams, and snails

1. Underline the question you must answer to solve the problem.

2. Underline the important facts in the Supporting Information.

3. List those facts:

    a. _____

    b. _____

    c. _____

4. Based on the facts, what would you predict are the best sessions for your class to attend? (Write them by session letter.) _____

5. For each of the choices, test your predictions by answering these questions:

    a. Will Session A help to complete the unit on ocean life?   ❏ yes   ❏ no
    b. Will Session B help to complete the unit?   ❏ yes   ❏ no
    c. Will Session C help to complete the unit?   ❏ yes   ❏ no
    d. Will Session D help to complete the unit?   ❏ yes   ❏ no
    e. Will Session E help to complete the unit?   ❏ yes   ❏ no

6. On a separate piece of paper, write reasons that tell why the sessions you chose are the best ones to help your class complete this study of ocean life.

62

Choosing the Correct Number Sequence

Directions: Read the problem carefully and then choose the number sentence that fits the problem. Write that answer on the appropriate line.

1. Alexi has 45 baseball cards. His brother, Leo, has 38. How many baseball cards do they have altogether?

   a. 45 - 38 = _____   b. 45 + 38 = _____   c. 38 + _____ = 45

2. Alexi has 64 baseball cards. His brother, Leo, has 95. How many more cards does Leo have than Alexi?

   a. 95 + 64 = _____   b. 64 - 95 = __   c. 95 - 64 = _____

3. Leo had some baseball cards. He gave 24 to his brother, Alexi. Leo then had 18 left. How many cards did Leo have to begin with?

   a. 24 - 18 = _____   b. 18 + 24 = _____   c. 24 - _____ = 18

4. Leo had some baseball cards. After he received 36 more from his brother, he had 87. How many baseball cards did Leo start with?

   a. 87 + 36 = _____   b. _____ - 36 = 87   c. 87 - 36 = _____

5. Alexi has 91 baseball cards. The complete collection is composed of 160 cards. How many more will he need to complete his collection?

   a. 160 - 91 = _____   b. 160 + 91 = _____   c. 91 - 160 = _____

6. Annie had six boxes of marbles. Each box had 12 marbles in it. How many marbles did Annie have?

   a. 12 + 6 = _____   b. 12 - 6 =_____   c. 12 x 6 = _____

7. Christina has 72 large marbles. They come in nine colorful boxes. How many marbles are there per box?

   a. 72 x 9 = _____   b. 72 + 9 = _____   c. 72 ÷ 9 = _____

8. Annie has 18 outfits. She has three times as many outfits as Christina. How many outfits does Christina have?

   a. 18 x 3 = _____   b. 18 ÷ 3 = _____   c. 18 - 3 = _____

9. Christina has 48 marbles. She put the same number of marbles in eight boxes. How many boxes did Christina use?

   a. 48 - 8 = _____   b. 48 ÷ 8 = _____   c. 48 x 8 = _____

10. Annie has seven blouses. Her sister, Christina, who is the same size as Annie, has six skirts. How many outfits do the sisters have if they share?

   a. 7 x 6 = _____   b. 7 + 6 = _____   c. 7 - 6 = _____

Underlining and Listing Facts

1. a. Draw a double line under the main fact in the problem below. Then draw a single line under each fact that supports the main fact.

    In cold weather, when the temperature drops below 32° F, water freezes. Rain turns to snow or sleet. Water on a window pane turns to frost. The surface of lakes and ponds turns to ice. When the temperature rises above 32°, these conditions change.

    b. Why? _____

    c. Based on the given facts below, underline the best conclusion:
    Given: Storm clouds are approaching. It will either rain or it will snow. The temperature has dropped to 20° F.
    Conclusion: It will probably rain.
                          It will probably snow.

2. Draw a double line under the main fact in the problem below. Then draw a single line under each fact that supports the main fact.

    Sam, Gertrude, Arnold, and Kim each play a different musical instrument. Two of the instruments are wind instruments—a flute and a trumpet. The other two are string instruments—a violin and a guitar. Arnold does not play the violin or flute. Kim does not play a wind instrument. Sam has been playing the guitar for five years. Who plays which instrument?

    List the facts you underlined on the lines below. Separate the main fact from the supporting facts.

    Main Fact: _____
    Supporting Facts: _____
    _____
    _____

    Conclusion: Based on the given facts, write the answers.
    _____ plays guitar.
    _____ plays trumpet.
    _____ plays the flute.
    _____ plays the violin.

Using Proof Format to Solve Problems

Directions: Use the following model to help you prove whether conclusions made from facts are true or false.

1. Vegetables grow from seeds. I enjoy my vegetable garden. My favorite vegetable to plant is summer squash.

   a. Find the main fact of the paragraph and write it in the IF box.

   b. Locate a specific fact related to the main fact and write it in the AND box.

   c. Use the information from the main fact IF and specific fact AND to write a concluding fact.

   d. Decide whether THEN is true or false.

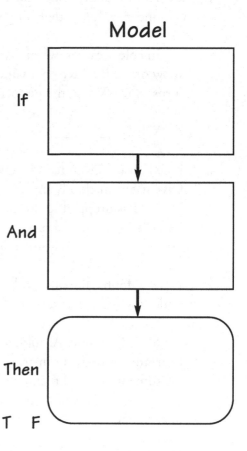

Model

If

And

Then

T   F

2. Gerbils, hamsters, and mice are all members of the rodent family. In our classroom we have two pets. They are Jake the gerbil and Holly the hamster. Are Jake and Holly rodents?　❑ yes　❑ no

   Write the two facts that prove your answer.

   If

   And

   Then

Using Analogies: Compare and Contrast

Directions: Complete each statement with the correct word.

1. Airplane is to sky as ship is to _____.

2. Key is to lock as knob is to _____.

3. Teacher is to school as _____ is to hospital.

4. Hangar is to airplane as garage is to _____.

5. Bird is to nest as lion is to _____.

6. Odor is to fragrance as _____ is to amazement.

7. China is to Asia as France is to _____.

8. Flat is to map as round is to _____.

9. Everest is to mountain as Pacific is to _____.

10. Snake is to _____ as whale is to mammal.

11. Water is to thirsty as food is to _____.

12. ↕ is to ↔ as vertical is to _____.

13. Vertical is to horizontal as longitude is to _____.

14. a + b is to b + a as x - y is to _____.

15. ▲ is to 1/4 as ◭ is to _____.

Choosing the Right Number from the Facts

Directions: Read the information given for each question below. Then fill in the blank with the single number that satisfies the given facts.

1. **Given that:**   Number x 5 = 0   Then the number is _____.
                 Number ÷ 3 = 0   3   8   5   0   16
                 Number + 8 = 8

2. **Given that:**   23 x Number = 23   Then the number is _____.
                 23 ÷ Number = 23   0   11   1   23   0
                 23 - Number = 22

3. **Given that:**   Number is between 9 and 18   Then the number is _____.
                 It is divisible by 3.   21   102   15   12   16
                 The sum of its digits is 3.

4. **Given that:**   Number is even.   Then the number is _____.
                 It is a multiple of 6.   6   30   13   66   24
                 Its ones digit is twice its tens digit.

5. **Given that:**   Number is odd.   Then the number is _____.
                 If 2 is added to it, it will   13   18   9   19   23
                     be divisible by 3.
                 It is greater than 3 x 5.

6. **Given that:**   The number is greater
        than 0 and less than 50.
    It is divisible by 3 and 5.
    It is even.

    Then the number is _____.
        6   15   10   30   45

7. **Given that:**   Mr. Wong has three daughters.
    Two of them are twins.
    The sum of all their ages is 65.
    The oldest daughter is 31.

    Then how old are the twins?
    _____

8. I am thinking of a number that is:
        even.
        between 30 and 50.
        a multiple of 4.
        The sum of its digits is odd.
        The sum of its digits is prime.

    The number I am thinking of
    is _____.

Finding Facts Using a Pie Chart

Directions: This delicious pizza was eaten by the Alfredo family. Use the diagram to answer the following questions:

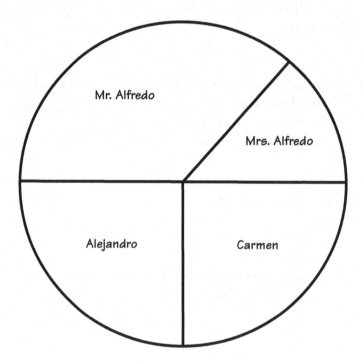

1. What fraction of the pizza did Carmen eat? _____

2. How much pizza did Mr. and Mrs. Alfredo have? _____

3. Who ate the least pizza? _____

4. How much did Mr. Alfredo have? _____

5. How much did Alejandro and Carmen have? _____

6. Is it possible from this pie chart to find out how much the pizza cost? _____

7. Is it possible to find out from the information given above if the pizza had pepperoni on it? _____

8. How would you have divided the pizza more evenly?
    I would have given each person _____ of the pizza.

Finding Facts Using a Bar Graph I

Police Emergency Calls

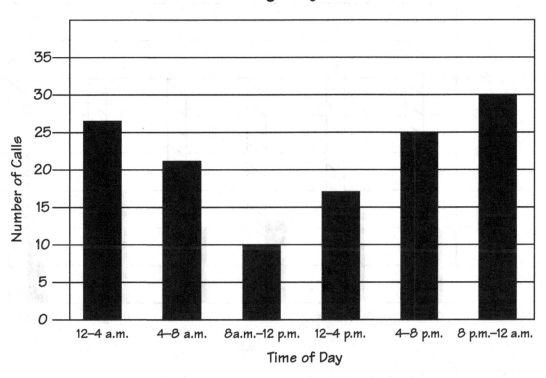

1. To which time period would you say the police chief should assign the most people? _____

2. When are the least number of police required? _____

3. If the chief assigns six police officers to the 8 a.m.–12 p.m. period, approximately how many should be assigned to the 8 p.m.–12 a.m. period? _____

4. Do most emergencies occur before or after 12 noon? _____

5. Between which two periods is there the greatest drop in police calls?_____

6. Does this table tell you precisely how many calls the Police Station received during the third hour of the afternoon? _____

7. Go to the counseling office of your school and find out how many students asked for help each day during the last month. Arrange your statistics for each day and see if there is a pattern. Then advise the counselor on which day of the week the office needs the most help.

Finding Facts Using a Bar Graph II

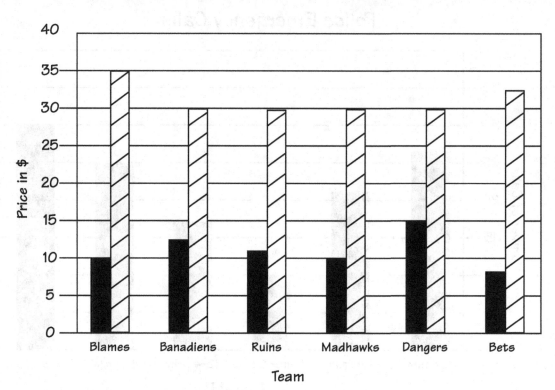

Team

■ Shows lowest price per ticket in the Big Six League

▨ Shows highest price per ticket in the Big Six League

SOURCE: *Big Six News*

1. What is the source of the above statistical table? _____

2. Name two teams whose least expensive tickets cost the same.

_____ and _____

3. Name two teams whose most expensive tickets cost over $30.00.

_____ and _____

4. Does this table tell you whether teams have any discounts for children? _____

5. What is the lowest cost of a ticket sold by the New York Dangers? _____

    The maximum cost? _____

6. What is the difference between the highest priced ticket and the lowest priced ticket sold
    by the Boston Ruins? _____

    _____

7. Which team has the most expensive ticket in the Big Six League?

    _____

    At what price? _____

8. Which team has the least expensive ticket in the Big Six League?

    _____

    At what price? _____

9. Mr. and Mrs. Lafleur of Montreal took their two children to see the Banadiens play
    against the visiting Madhawks. If they spent $10 for parking and $8 for hot dogs, how
    much did they spend in all if they bought the least expensive tickets?

    _____

10. What is the average cost of the most expensive ticket in the Big Six League?

    _____

Using Facts to Construct Graphs

1. Directions: Use the facts below to complete the bar graph.

The ferris wheel costs three tickets.
The roller coaster costs five tickets.
The merry-go-round costs two tickets.
The bumper cars cost four tickets.

The round-up costs five tickets.
The giant slide costs seven tickets
The haunted house costs three tickets

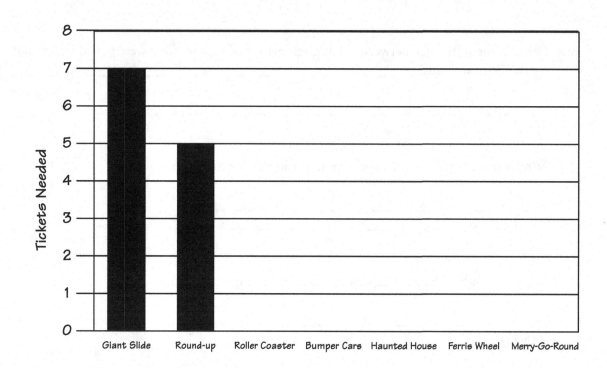

Using Facts to Construct Graphs *(Cont.)*

2. Directions: Use the information in the following paragraph to help you determine snowfall in six cities. Write each city's name on the bar graph.

The six cities are: **Pitt, Ainge, Baltic, Clarke, Dors, and Marse.**
Baltic had the greatest amount of snowfall in the five-year period. Ainge and Clarke had identical amounts of snowfall. With 60 feet of snow, Marse had the second greatest snowfall. Pitt had the least amount of snow in the five-year period.

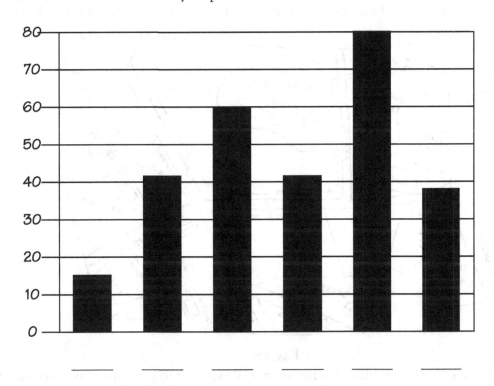

Using Facts and a Map to Solve Problems

The town of Skyhook has a trash problem. For years, people have taken care of their own trash. The result is that some areas have become littered and polluted. Today, a serious health problem is developing.

The town has set aside money to construct a dump site to be maintained by town workers. The main question is: On which of the three sites should the dump be located?

Use the map and the information given to conclude where the dump should be: Town Site A, Town Site B, or Town Site C. Write one statement telling why you would not vote for the other two sites.

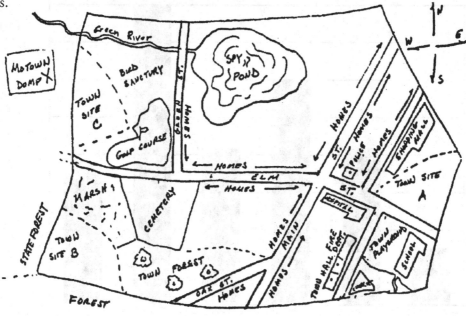

FACTS

• Skyhook spends considerable sums of money each year to keep Spy Pond a recreational area for swimming, fishing, and picnicking.

• Most homes are located off Elm and Main Streets.

• The neighboring town of Motown has its dump near Green River.

• Many school students cut through Town Site A on their way to school.

• Only ten houses are south of Elm Street and west of Main Street.

1. On what site would you place the dump? _____

2. What is the reason you did not choose the other two sites?

    _____

    _____

    _____

Using Facts and Tables or Diagrams

Directions: Solve the problems below by completing the table. Use an X for no and an O for yes.

1. Mrs. Finch, Mr. Peters, and Miss Kelly are teachers in our school. One is the librarian. one is the art teacher, and one is the gym instructor. Mrs. Finch does not work in the art room or in the library. Miss Kelly is not the librarian. What is each teacher's job?

Job	Librarian	Art Teacher	Gym Instructor
Mrs. Finch			
Mr. Peters			
Miss Kelly			

Mrs. Finch is the _____.
Mr. Peters is the _____.
Miss Kelly is the _____.

2. The Pyramids, the Squares, and the Octagons are the names of three musical groups. They play rock, jazz, and classical music, but not in that order. The rock group is not named after a three-dimensional geometric figure. The jazz group has eight members and is named after an eight-sided geometric figure. What kind of music does each musical group play?

Type of Music	Rock	Jazz	Classical
△			
■			
⬡			

The Pyramids play _____.
The Squares play _____.
The Octagons play _____.

3. The members of the 37th Street Fifth-Grade Club are Mack, Pete, Sam, and Mike. Mack is Mike's brother. The boys decided to have an election to determine who would be the leader of the club. Before the election, Peter said he would not vote for anyone whose name begins with the letter "M."

   The rules of the election were:
   (1) Each member casts one vote.
   (2) You cannot vote for yourself.
   (3) You cannot vote for your brother.

   After the election, the club members knew that Sam got only one vote, but who won the election? _____

VOTES RECEIVED

VOTERS		Mack	Peter	Sam	Mike
	Mack				
	Peter				
	Sam				
	Mike				

4. Six members of the Prime football team are in a huddle. Their positions are: quarterback, running back, tight end, wide receiver, blocker, and kicker.

   a. The quarterback, who wore number 7, was directly across from the running back.
   b. The wide receiver was between the quarterback and the tight end.
   c. In the huddle, the kicker stood opposite the tight end, who had the running back to his right.

   Who wore number 17? _____

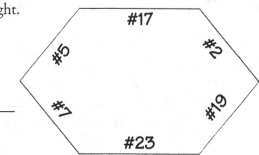

Book 8 • Grade 5

Special Techniques and Strategies

73

Making a Table to Solve a Problem I

Mr. Paterna purchased 20 yards of fencing to build a corral for Lisa's pet goat. Lisa thought that the goat would be happiest if the corral enclosed the greatest amount of area, allowing her pet to feed on the most grass possible. She wants to tell Mr. Paterna the right dimensions. Can you help her figure this out? Remember, Lisa has only 20 yards of fencing that she can use, so the perimeter will always be 20. First, complete this table.

Possible Sizes for the Corral

Length	1 yd	2	3				
Width	9 yds	8	7				
Perimeter (2W + 2 L)	20 yds	20	20	20	20	20	20
Area (L x W)	9 sq. yds	16					
	a.	b.	c.	d.	e.	f.	g.

1. Which dimensions will give Lisa's goat the greatest area? _____ x _____
2. Which dimensions will give it the least area?_____ x _____
3. What do you call the figure that has the same length and width? _____
   Which column describes this figure? _____

4. Which geometric shape do the dimensions in column **b.** give you? _____

    _____

5. Which columns in your table have the same area?

    Cols. _____ and _____ have _____ sq. yds.

    Cols. _____ and _____ have _____ sq. yds.

6. Were columns **f.** and **g.** necessary? _____

7. If Mr. Paterna had purchased 60 yards of fencing, what would the dimensions of the corral that enclosed the largest area be?
    (Hint: Make a similar chart with perimeter of 60.)

    Length_____ Width _____

8. If Lisa wanted to give her pet a maximum area of 81 square yards to play in, how much fencing should she buy? _____

    _____

74

Making a Table to Solve a Problem II

Directions: Read the problem. Then use the questions on page 4 to help you fill in the table.

The town of Salisbury, CT needs 23 pounds of cement for basketball courts in the park. The Salisbury Hardware Store is having a sale:

What combination of 3- and 7-lb. bags should the town buy to obtain 23 lbs. at the lowest cost?

You can solve this problem by making a table:

7 lb. bags	Cost per bag	Total Cost	3 lb. bags	Cost per bag	Total Cost	Total in lbs.	TOTAL COST
4			0			28+0=28	$
3			1				
1							

1. How many pounds are needed in all?_____

Fill in the first line of your table:

2. 4 bags x $4.25 per bag = $ _____
3. 4 bags x 7 lbs. = _____ lbs.

Fill in the second line of your table:

4. 3 bags x 7 lbs. = _____ lbs.
5. 1 bag x 3 lbs. = _____ lbs.
6. Total amount in lbs. in line 2 is _____.
7. Total dollar amount in line 2 is _____.

Fill in the third line of your table:

8. To get exactly 23 lbs., you could buy _____ 7-lb. bags and _____ 3-lb. bags.
9. This will cost $ _____.

Fill in the fourth line of your table:

10. Is it cheaper to buy only one 7-lb. bag and six 3-lb. bags? _____
11. According to your chart, which is the best combination? _____

_____

75

Guess and Test I

It costs $.50 to buy an angelfish and $.32 to buy a goldfish. When Ellie got home from the pet store, she told her Mom she bought 14 fish for a total of $5.56.

How many angelfish and how many goldfish did Ellie buy?

Hint: Could Ellie have bought 10 angelfish?

Then my first guess should be (choose one):

a. less than 10;   or   b. greater than 10.

Now, make a table:

Angelfish $0.50		Goldfish $0.32		TOTALS	
Number	Cost	Number	Cost	Number	Cost
9	$4.50	5	$1.60	14	$6.10

Ellie bought _____ angelfish and
_____ goldfish.

Guess and Test II

1. Fill in the numbers 1, 2, 3, 4, 5. Each line of numbers, the line across and the line up and down, must add up to 10.

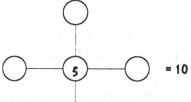

2. Fill in the numbers 1, 2, 3, 4, 5, 6. Each side of the triangle must add up to nine.

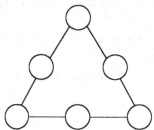

From the answers given below, choose the one that will make the open sentence true. Write that number in the blank.

3. 3 x _____ + 16 = 52

     33   9   10   12   8

4. 18 x _____ - 93 = 213

     1234   12   17   23   58

5. 9472 ÷ _____ - 52 = 96

     30   52   86   64   42

Hint: Use estimating to solve problems 6 and 7.

6. $3\frac{4}{9}$ x _____ = $18\frac{17}{18}$

     8     $5\frac{1}{2}$ 3   7 $4\frac{1}{2}$

7. $6\frac{2}{5}$ x _____ = $11\frac{1}{2}$

     $\frac{5}{8}$ $1\frac{1}{8}$ $2\frac{1}{8}$ $1\frac{3}{8}$ $1\frac{7}{8}$

Looking for Patterns

1. Directions: Read the problem carefully, observe the pattern, and then write the next element.

a. 800, 400, 200, 100, _____

b.   _____

c. ½, ¾, ⅚, ⅞, _____

d.

  2 pts   3 pts   4 pts   5 pts
  2 regions   4 regions   8 regions   _____ regions

e. Nixon, Ford, Carter, Reagan, _____

f. 2, 11, 20, 29, _____

g. 0, 1, 1, 2, 3, 5, 8, _____

h. 2, 5, 10, 17,_____

i. , , , _____ , _____

2. Directions: Below, the diagram on the left indicates the factoring of 30. The diagram on the right indicates the factoring of A. Find the value of A.

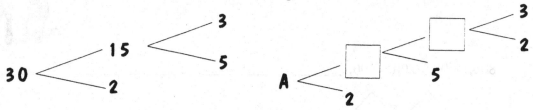

A = _____

3.   Complete the factoring of 1,050.

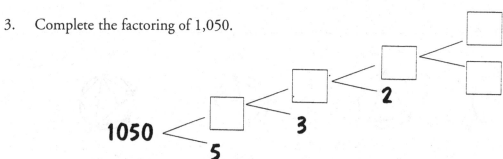

4.   A diagonal is a slanted line that connects two angles. How many diagonals are there in a dodecagon (12 sides)?

    a.   You can draw one, of course, and count the diagonals.   *OR*

    b.   You can reduce the problem, organize a list, and look for a pattern.

# sides	Figure	# diagonals
3	△	0
4	⊠	2
5		5
6		9
7		14
___		___
___		___
___		___
___		___

Answer: 12

Triangle Dot-Numbers

Directions: Look at the lst, 2nd, and 3rd triangle numbers below and observe the patterns. Complete the chart for 4th–7th triangle numbers. Then answer the questions on page 10

Triangle Number	Dots in form of a Triangle	Sum of Dots	Think
1st	• ••	3	(2 + 1)
2nd	3↓ •• ↗1 •••• →2	6	(3 + 2 + 1)
3rd	• •• ••• ••••	10	(4 + 3 + 2 + 1)
4th			
5th			
6th			
7th			

Triangle Dot-Numbers *(Cont.)*

1. How many dots does the lst triangle number have on each side? _____

2. How many dots does the 2nd triangle number have on each side?
   The 3rd triangle? _____

3. How many dots would the 10th triangle number have on each side? _____

4. Therefore, how many dots would the *nth* triangle number have on each side? _____
   The 753rd triangle number? _____

5. Trace the dots around the perimeter of the 4th triangle. Then count the dots
   inside. _____ dots (Notice that this equals the lst triangle number!)

6. Trace the dots around the perimeter of your 5th triangle. How many dots does it have
   inside? _____ (Notice that this equals the 2nd triangle number!)

7. Therefore, how many dots would the 8th triangle have inside? (It will be the same as the
   sum of dots for the_____
   triangle number)_____ dots

8. What triangle number would result if one traces the perimeter of the *nth* triangle number? _____

9. Therefore, if one traces the perimeter of the 650th triangle number, _____
   the _____triangle number will result.

10. How are the numbers in the "sum of dots" column on page 9 changing? _____
    _____

Square Dot-Numbers

Directions: Study the table of the square dot-numbers. Observe the patterns, complete the table, and then answer the questions.

Square Numbers	Dot Form	Sum of Dots	Think	Symbol
1 square	●	1	1 x 1	$1^{\square}$ (1^2)
2 square	●● ●●	4	2 x 2	$2^{\square}$ (2^2)
3 square	●●● ●●● ●●●	9	3 x 3	$3^{\square}$ (3^2)
4 square				
5 square				
6 square				

1. How many dots would a $50^{\square}$ (50^2) number have altogether?

   x _____ =

2. How many dots would a $100^{\square}$ (100^2) number have on each side?

3. How many dots does each of these square numbers have around its perimeter?
   a. $3^{\square}$: _____ dots   c. $5^{\square}$: _____ dots
   b. $4^{\square}$: _____ dots   d. $6^{\square}$: _____ dots

4. Observe the pattern. How many dots would the $7^{\square}$ number have around its perimeter?
   _____ dots

5. How many dots do you think the $10^{\square}$ number would have around its perimeter?
   _____ dots

Square Dot-Numbers: Tracing

Directions: Study the table of the square dot-numbers and their traced perimeter. Notice the patterns, complete the table, and then answer the questions.

Square Numbers	Traced Perimeter	Number of Dots Inside
2 square	☐	0
3 square		1^2
4 square		2^2
5 square		
6 square		
7 square		

1. Observe the patterns of the first and last columns of the table above. How many dots will the traced 50-square (50^2) number have inside? _____

2. Therefore, the traced n-square number must have _____ dots inside.

3. The traced 750-square number must have _____ dots inside.

Counting Figures

A. The Mexican Hat Triangle Problem
Directions: Count the triangles in the Mexican hat below.

Hint: Name the triangular regions with letters as shown below and make an organized list:

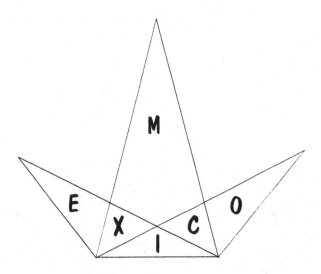

1.   One-region triangles: _____

2.   Two-region triangles: _____

3.   Three-region triangles: _____

4.   Four-region triangles: _____

5.   Five-region triangles: _____

6.   Therefore, the total number of triangles in the Mexican hat is _____

Counting Figures *(Cont.)*

B. Star Triangle Problem
Directions: Name each triangular region in the star below with a letter or a number.

How many triangles are there?

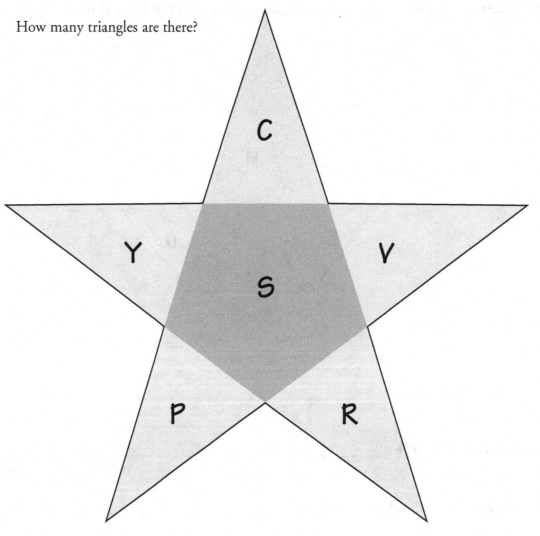

1. One-region triangles (use your notations): _____

2. Two-region triangles: _____

3. Three-region triangles: _____

4. Four-region triangles: _____

5. Therefore, the total number of triangles in the star is _____

82

Tiling

Grace is going to tile her bathroom floor with square tiles all one unit in length. She decided to call the figures she was making polyominoes. The following figures are three examples of poly-ominoes:

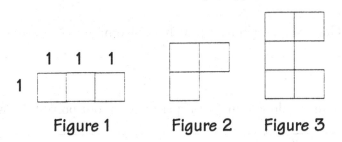

Figure 1   **Figure 2**   **Figure 3**

1.   What is the area of Figure 2? _____

2.   What is the perimeter of Figure 3? _____

3.   What will the area be if Grace adds a tile to Figure 1? _____
     The perimeter? _____

4.   If Grace had a 25-tile polyomino, what would the new area be if she added one
     more tile? _____

5.   Can you add a tile to Figure 2 and have the perimeter stay the same? What will the new
     diagram look like? _____

6.   Add a tile to Figure 3 so that the perimeter will increase by two units. What will the new
     polyomino look like? _____

7.   Where should Grace attach the next tile on Figure 3 so that the perimeter will actually
     <u>decrease</u>? Draw the resulting polyomino.

8. If Grace started with just one tile, could she, by adding new tiles, get

    a. A perimeter of three? _____   b. A perimeter of five? _____

    c. A perimeter of seven? _____   d. A perimeter of nine?_____

9. Do you think Grace will ever come up with a polyomino that has an odd
   perimeter? _____

10. What kind of numbers do you think the perimeter of our polyomino will always
    be? _____

11. **Conjectures**:

    a. If the tile you add has only one side in common with the polyomino, then the
       perimeter always _____ by _____.

    b. If the tile you add has two sides in common with the polyomino, then the perimeter
       always _____.

    c. If the tile you add has three sides in common with the polyomino, then the perimeter
       always _____ by _____.

12. Can you create a polyomino whose area is 5? _____ 19? _____.

    Does the area always increase by one when you add a tile?_____

Book 9 · Grade 5

Combinations, Ratios, and Thinking Ahead

83

Finding Combinations

1. For camp, Janice packed three shirts: one blue, one green, and one red, together with two pairs of slacks: one blue and one white. List the different shirt-slacks outfits she can wear.

Shirt - Slacks Combinations

blue-blue

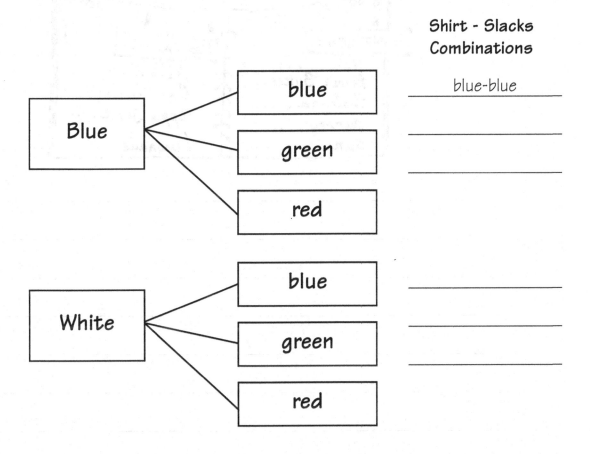

How many outfit combinations are there? _____

2. The U.S. Military Academy offers its young recruits training in computers, mechanics, or economics. Graduates can then work for the Army, Air Force, Navy, or Marines. How many academic-military careers are possible?

    Make a table on a separate sheet of paper, as in Example 1, and list the possibilities.

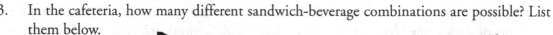

3. In the cafeteria, how many different sandwich-beverage combinations are possible? List them below.

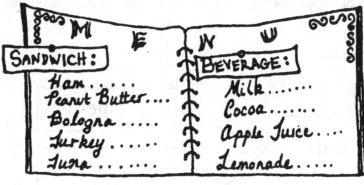

_____

_____

_____

_____

_____

_____

_____

4. At the bookstore, Donald decided to get his friend, Andrew, two books for his birthday. He wanted to buy one mystery volume and one biography of a U.S. President. How many different mystery-biography gift combinations are possible?

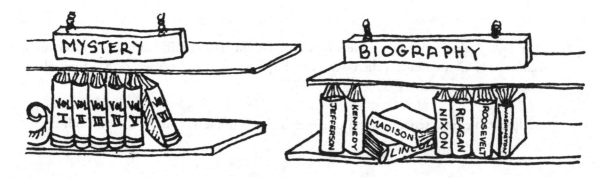

Finding Ratios I

Directions: The ratio between two numbers is a fraction, stated in lowest terms: 6 to 8 is 6/8 = 3/4, or 3:4. Ratios are important because they help us compare numbers. Circle the correct answer in each of these problems.

1. If the ratio of A to B is 1, then
    a. A > B   b. A < B   c. A = B

2. If the ratio of A to B is less than 1, then
    a. A > B   b. A < B   c. A = B

3. If the ratio of A to B is greater than 1, then
    a. A > B   b. A < B   c. A = B

4. When it comes to gold, jewelers consider pure gold to be 24-karat.

    a. What is the ratio of 14-karat gold to pure gold?_____

    _____

    b. What is the ratio of 18-karat gold to pure gold?_____

    _____

5. When it comes to silver, jewelers consider 1000-silver to be pure silver.

a. What is the ratio of 925-silver to pure silver?_____

    _____

b. Which has the higher silver content, 925-silver (sterling) or 800-silver (Oriental silver)?

    _____

6. Mrs. Helm wants to prepare some punch for Jonathan's party. The directions on the can state that she should add one can of concentrate to three cans of cold water to make 1/2 gallon of punch.

    a. What is the ratio of water to concentrate? _____

    b. How many cans of concentrate will Mrs. Helm have to buy to make one gallon of punch? _____

    c. How many cans of water will Mrs. Helm use to make two gallons of punch? _____

    _____

7. For every $.25 newspaper that Lisa, delivers she is allowed to keep $.05.

    a. What is the ratio of the money kept versus the money collected if Lisa delivered only one newspaper? _____

    b. How much money did Lisa keep if she sold 50 newspapers in one afternoon? _____

    _____

    c. How much money did Lisa keep if she collected $20.00 on Saturday? _____

    _____

    d. How much money did Lisa return to the newspaper company if she sold 100 newspapers by the end of the week? _____

85

Finding Ratios II

1. Let us observe the side-to-area (S: A) ratio of a square.

Think

a. **1**
   1

S : A is  which is ___1___ : ___1___

b. **2**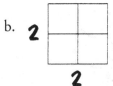
   2

S : A is  which is _____ : _____

c. **4**
   4

S : A is  which is _____ : _____

d. **8**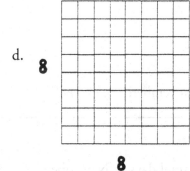
   8

S : A is  which is _____ : _____

We can conclude, then, if you: (circle one)
     increase the side of the square by 1
     double the side of the square
     increase the side of the square by 2

then you (circle one)
     increase the area by 1
     increase the area by 4
     increase the area times 4.

2. The school calendar shows that, in November, the students have three vacation days.

    They are:
    Veterans' Day – November 11
    Thanksgiving Break – November 28 and 29

    a. What is the ratio of school days to total days in November?

    _____

    b. What is the ratio of total days off from school to total days in November?

    _____

    c. What is the ratio of vacation days to total school days in November?

    _____

    d. What is the ratio of total days off from school to total school days in November?

    _____

86

Comparing Probabilities

Directions: The more likely it is for an event to occur, the higher the probability. Knowing the probability of an event occurring can help you make better decisions and predict the outcome of events. In the questions below, check the one more likely to occur.

1. _____ snow in August or
   _____ snow in January?

2. _____ good grades when you do your homework or
   _____ good grades when you watch TV?

3. _____ correct guess on a five-choice quiz or
   _____ correct guess on a three-choice quiz?

4. _____ striking out if your batting average is .327 or
   _____ striking out if your batting average is .169?

5. _____ becoming a college graduate or
   _____ becoming a professional athlete?

6. _____ drawing a queen from a deck of cards or
   _____ drawing a card with hearts on it from a deck of cards?

7. _____ pulling the letter P from an alphabet or
   _____ pulling a vowel from an alphabet?

8. _____ seeing a seagull at the beach or
   _____ seeing a robin at the beach?

9. _____ being elected President of the U.S. or
   _____ being elected President of France?

10. _____ an event with 1/5 probability or
    _____ an event with 3/5 probability?

What Are the Chances? I

1. In a box full of baseballs, what are the chances of your finding a soccer ball?_____
    _____

    That is to say, the probability of finding a soccer ball in a box full of baseballs is

    _____.

2. If you picked up a ball from a box full of soccerballs, what are the chances that it will be a
    soccer ball? _____

    That is to say, the probability of finding a soccer ball in a box full of soccerballs is

    _____. It is a sure thing.

3. These black and white balls are
    placed in a hat.

    a. Is there a higher probability of choosing a black ball or a white ball
        from the hat? _____

    b. What is the probability of choosing a white ball?_____

    c. What is the probability of choosing a black ball? _____

What Are the Chances? II

1. The names of eight students are placed in a hat. They are:

Amy	Ellen
Ben	Steve
Susan	Sara
Sam	Ellie

a. Is there a higher probability of picking a boy's name or girl's name from the hat?

_____

b. What is the probability of picking a boy's name?

_____

c. What is the probability of picking a girl's name?

_____

d. Is there a higher probability of picking a name that begins with the letter S or a name that beings with the letter E?

_____

e. What is the probability of picking a name that begins with the letter S?

_____

f. What is the probability of picking a name that begins with the letter E?

_____

g. What is the probability of picking Ellen's name?

_____

2.   Usually a packet of baseball cards contains 16 cards and costs $1.00.

    a.   In a league where you have 320 players, what are the chances of your finding a Billy Ripken if you bought one packet?

    _____

    b.   If you spend $2.00 buying baseball cards, what are your chances of finding a Jose Canseco?

    _____

    c.   If Peter spent $20.00 and bought the entire 1989 set of baseball players with 320 cards in it, what is the probability that Peter will find an Orel Hershiser?

    _____

    d.   How much money should you spend to be sure that you will find a Dwight Gooden?

    _____

3.   If you toss a coin, what are the odds it will come up heads?

    _____

That is to say, the probability of getting heads when tossing a coin is the fraction_____

_____.

89

Probability Spinner

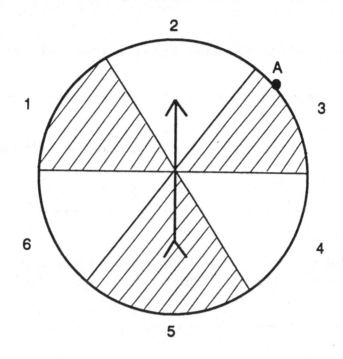

1. In the spinner above, what is the probability of the arrow stopping in region 5?

   _____

2. What is the probability of the arrow stopping in region 6?

   _____

3. What is the probability of the arrow stopping in regions 2 or 3?

   _____

4. What is the probability of the arrow stopping in a shaded area?

   _____

5. What do you think the probability of the arrow stopping at point A is going to be
   Choose one:

   _____ very, very small
   _____ small
   _____ large
   _____ sure thing

6. What is the probability of the arrow stopping in a region with numbers greater than 2?

   _____

7. What is the probability of the arrow stopping in a region with numbers less than or equal to 2?

   _____

8. If you added up the probabilities of the arrow stopping in region 1, region 2, region 3, region 4, region 5, and region 6, what will the total probability be?

   _____

9. If P (1) is the probability of the arrow stopping in region 1, what is P (6) equal to?

   _____

10. What is P (black)?

   _____

11. What is P (white)?

   _____

12. What is P (black or white)?

   _____

90

Thinking Ahead: The Big Picture

Directions: Look at the overall picture, think, and zero in on a possible solution. The first one is done for you.

1. 2 x 4 x 6 x 8 x 10 x 12 x 14 x 16 x 0 = <u>0</u>

    If you look at the entire problem before beginning to multiply, you will see that the answer has to be zero.

2. What answer do you get when you multiply:
    1/4 x 1/3 x 1/2 x 1 x 2 x 3 x 4 = _____

3. A train leaves Philadelphia at noon traveling at 60 m.p.h. toward New York. Another train leaves New York for Philadelphia at 2 p.m. at 70 m.p.h. How far apart are the trains when they meet? _____

4. Can you predict the number that goes in the square with the circle in the following diagram?

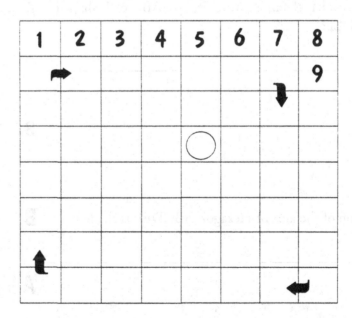

Hint: How many small squares does the big square contain? _____
Mark the square that is the last one. Then subtract to find the number that goes in the circle.

5. What fraction of the area of the circle is shaded?

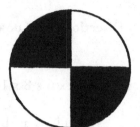

_____

6. What fraction of the area of the big square is shaded?

_____

7. Which diagram has the most area, Triangle ABC or L-shaped figure ABCDEF?

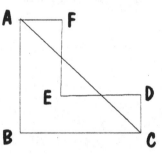

_____

8. What fraction of the area of Hexagon ABCDEF is shaded?

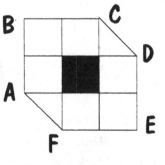

_____

Answer Key

☞ Answer Key

Lesson 1, Pages 15–16

In teaching the section, emphasize the "key" words that will trigger in the child's mind the appropriate number sentence. In the case of number 1, 8 + 6 _____?

1. How many altogether?
2. How much more does Leo need?
3. How many more days before (the family leaves)?
4. How old is Tom?
5. What time will the train arrive?
6. Who was the Red Sox fan?
7. How much (money) did I have to start with?
8. Who has the longer ride?
9. Who counted correctly?
10. What was the Patriot's point total at half-time?

Lesson 2, Pages 17–18

1. c
2. b   (all but three are the key words).
3. a
4. c
5. b
   (Children do not need to know what area is. Just by examining the words bigger and smaller, a student will probably choose b.)

Lesson 3, Pages 19–20

1. b
2. a
3. c
4. a
5. c

Lesson 4, Pages 21–22

1. Why did the cashier give Andrew $.50?
2. Why were the farmers happy in July?
3. Who is the oldest brother?
4. What is the difference that makes Terrific Tonic a better buy than Supersoda?

Lesson 5, Page 23

1. a. Tom is seven years older than Bill.
   b. Bill is eight years old.
2. a. Boards cost $45.00.
   b. Nails cost $5.00.
   c. Paint costs $15.00.
3. a. He has been given 15 problems.
   b. He has done eight.
4. a. One pencil for $.59.
   b. Two notebooks for $3.00 each.
   c. One eraser for $.31.
5. a. Sue and Maria earned $12.00.
   b. Sue's share was $8.00.

Lesson 6, Page 24

1. a. The baseball glove costs $14.00.
   b. Leo's allowance is $2.00 per week.
2. a. Phyllis had $10.00.
   b. She saved $3.00.
   c. Phyllis spent $5.00.
3. a. Nancy was absent six times during the year.
   b. Award is given to children who have missed no more than one week of school.
   Note: The assumption here is that the school week is five days.
4. Roger practices 30 minutes per day.
5. a. Book has 48 pages.
   b. Jeremiah read 20 pages.

Answer Key

Lesson 7, Page 25

2. d
3. b
4. d
5. d

Lesson 8, Pages 26–27

1. a. Friday
   b. Four times a month (once a week)
2. a. Tuesday
   b. Two times a month
3. On Wednesday; every two weeks
4. On the 12–14 weekend
5. On the 19th
6. By Thursday, October 3

Lesson 9, Pages 28–29

1. October 10
2. Antiques and Crafts Show
3. 7 a.m.
4. Marshfield Fairgrounds
5. No, remember, the public is welcome.
6. $15.00
7. Nothing: "Under 12 Free"
8. South Shore Rotary Club
9. a. $2.00
   b. 0
   c. $2.00
   d. $2.00
   e. $6.00
10. Crafts section

Lesson 10, Pages 30–31

1. a. F
   b. T
   c. ING
   d. F
2. a. ING
   b. T
   c. F
   d. T
3. a. ING
   b. T
   c. ING
   d. F
4. a. F
   b. T
   c. T
   d. ING
5. a. F
   b. ING
   c. T
   d. ING
6. a. T
   b. ING
   c. T
   d. ING
7. a. ING
   b. ING
   c. T
   d. F

Lesson 11, Pages 32–33

1. c
2. b
3. b
4. b
5. a
6. c
7. c
8. b

☞ Answer Key

Lesson 12, Page 37
1. a. yellow
   b. red
   c. green
2. It went up to 55° by noon.
   15° was the difference.

Lesson 13, Page 38

1. November
2. 24"
3. 15"
4. December, January
5. February had 9"

Lesson 14, Pages 39–40

1. three items
2. five items
3. three items
4. $.25
5. two items
6. four sports items
7. three school items
8. eraser, pen, nails, tennis ball, hammer, shovel, soccer ball, bat, book, mitt.

Lesson 15, Pages 41–42

1. a. North St ‹ Main St. ‹ South St.
   b. North St. ‹ Oak St. ‹ South St.
   c. North St. ‹ Main St. ‹ South St.
   d. North St. ‹ Oak St. ‹ South St.
2. Yes; North St. ‹ Oak St. ‹ South St. (shortest distance)
3. a. No
   b. No
4. East
5. South

Lesson 16, Page 43

1. Three blocks away (Students' answers may vary depending on the direction they count.)
   a. A-B-D-C
   b. A-D-C
   c. nine miles
   d. 14 miles of fencing
   e. 23 miles

Lesson 17, Page 44

1. 7 hours; 5 ½ hours
2. a. 12 legs
   b. beetle
   c. four ants
   d. 30 legs
   e. ii

Lesson 18, Page 45

1. foot
2. white
3. cat
4. bird
5. bat
6. boy
7. sew
8. light
9. nest
10. hen

Lesson 19. Pages 46–47

1. □   2.

3. ▨   4. ⬠

Answer Key

Lesson 19. Pages 46–47 continued

5.   6.

7.   8.

9. 321
10. 6 x 8

Lesson 20, Pages 48–49

2. 6 gallons: 8, 24, 32
3. 30 quarts: 30, 42, 54
4. 3 miles: 40 min., 60 min., 80 min., 100 min., 120 mins. (2 hrs.)
5. 36 cookies: 9, 18) 27, 36, 45
6. five

tomatoes	1	2	3	4	5
spoiled	5	10	15	20	25

Lesson 21, Pages 50–51

A.

1. a. fur
   b. yes; all cats have fur, Hector is a (skinny) cat, (Hector likes to climb) (trees). (Also, Hector is skinny.)
2. a. of "converse:"
       All cats have fur.
       Hector is a cat.
       Hector has fur.
       but
       All spiders have eight legs.
       An octopus has eight legs.
       An octopus is not a spider.

Note: In 1a, Hector is a member of the set of cats. Since "all cats have fur," it follows that Hector has fur. In 2a, octopus is not a member of the set of spiders. Therefore, even though it has eight legs like a spider, it is not necessarily a spider.

   b. No. (The idea of counter example: An octopus is an animal with eight legs and it is not a spider.)

B.
2. True
3. False (He could own a Ford truck.)
4. False
5. False
6. True
7. False
8. False
9. False
10. False

Lesson 22, Pages 55–56

1. a. 80   b. 50   c. 30
   d. 70   e. 60   f. 50
   g. 20   h. 20   I. 70
   j. 70   k. 10   1. 90
   m. 10   n. 30   o. 10
   p. 40   q. 10   r. 20
   s. 140   t. 640
2. a. 200   b. 600   c. 500
   d. 100   e. 300   f. 800
   g. 300   h. 700   i. 400
   j. 600   k. 100   l. 500
   m. 800   n. 300   o. 100
   p. 400   q. 900   r. 600
   s. 1900 t. 2900
3. a. Just below or "about" $1.80.
   b. Just below $.90.

Lesson 22, Pages 55–56, continued

3. c. Just below $1.60.
   d. Just above $.40.
   e. Above $3.00.
   f. About $1.60 (precisely, this time).
   g. About $1.20.
   h. About $2.80.
   i. About $2.70.
   j. Less than $3.00.

Lesson 23, Pages 57–58

1. 20
2. Of course, answers will vary. "15 pencils, so it must be about 30 inches long," for example.
3. five
4. nine
5. 400
6. below

Note: The ability to estimate is an essential skill. The idea in question 1 can, of course, be extended to say, "How many people are watching the Yankees at Yankee Stadium?" A child can choose a section of the stands, count the people in it and then multiply by the number of sections around the stadium and come up with an estimate. The mathematical notion that multiplication is an efficient way to do addition is introduced here. To extend question 2, hand the children a pencil, have them measure it in inches (round it off to the whole inch) and have them estimate the different furniture in the classroom in lengths in "pencils."

In 3 and 4, division is the primary operation. One has to go to five boxes of spaghetti to feed the two extra people, since four will not be enough. A colleague of mine insists that "A little bit too much is just enough, especially when it comes to spaghetti …"

7. 45
8. 20
9. eight
10. two

Lesson 24, Pages 59–60

2. c
3. c. Note: In 3, all we are interested in is the logic. If it takes one of them two hours to finish the job, two of them working together should take less than two hours.
4. a
5. c
6. b. Note: Here the student should expect the answer to be less then $30.00. Students do not need to know what 20% really means. This is a gentle way to introduce concepts that traditionally students have trouble with.
7. c
8. a
9. b. 20 feet (Swing will be about 3' off the ground and allowance must be made for rope to go over the branch and be secured under the swing.)
10. b. 12:00
11. b. five
12. a. eight blocks
13. c. eight trips
14. b. halved

☞ Answer Key

Lesson 25, Pages 61–63

1.	+	14.	+
2.	-	15.	-
3.	x	16.	+
4.	÷	17.	-
5.	+	18.	-
6.	x	19.	÷
7.	÷	20.	x
8.	-	21.	subtract
9.	+	22.	subtract
10.	+	23.	multiply
11.	-	24.	divide
12.	x	25.	divide
13.	x	26.	add

Lesson 26, Page 64

1. $5.00
2. $2.00
3. $.22
4. 14 years
5. Robert, by two hours
6. $6.00
7. 18 feet, or half-way down.
8. three
9. 15,750

Lesson 27, Page 65

1. two miles
2. four balls
3. $45.00
4. seven (two years passed)
5. 0 pigeons (13 flew away when Tony frightened them by catching 5)
6. 13 flew away
7. 15 points

Lesson 28, Pages 66–67

1. a. four
   b. four (red-green; blue-white; red-blue; green-white)
   c. one total: nine in all
2. a. three
   b. four (black-green; purple-red; black-purple; green-red)
   c. one
   Total: eight in all
3. three triangles: ABD, DBC, ABC
4. GHKF, FKDE, HABK, KBCD, GACE
5. ABC, CBD, ABD
6. two squares; five triangles
7. five triangles

Lesson 29, Pages 68–69

2. 9 + 9 + 9 + 9 = 36
   Note: The idea here is to force the child to look at the overall picture; observe a pattern of pairing; find a value for each pair (9) and then add, gaining speed in doing mental calculations. The next step, of course is:

   Find a value for each pair.
   Count the numbers of pairs.
   Multiply
   In 2: Value of each pair is: 9
   Number of pairs if: x 4
   The answer is: 36
3. 14 + 14 + 14 = 42
4. 5 + 10 + 10 = 25
   If you have an odd number to add, simply add the middle number to the result you get after pairing and multiplying.

Lesson 29, Pages 68–69, continued

Value of each pair is: 10
Number of pairs is: x 2
        20
then add: 5
to get: 25

With repeated practice using this method, the child will see multiplication as the most efficient way to do addition.

5. $13 + 13 + 13 + 13 + 13 + 13 = 78$

Lesson 30, Page 70

2. 9s; $4 \times 9 = 36$
3. 13s; $3 \times 13 = 39$

Lesson 31, Page 73

1. What is the difference between a 15-foot by 15-foot square and a 9-foot by 9-foot square? Although the student only has to rephrase the question, one could draw a diagram on the board and ask a volunteer to "color" in what the question is asking.

   With the visual aid, the concept of the square is reinforced, and the answer is in square units. A student might also rephrase the question as, "How much floor is showing after you lay the rug down?" If time allows, one might also point out that the underlining concept of the question is area.

2. Who started raking first, Maria or Jeff? or Who has been raking longer, Maria or Jeff?
3. How much money did John spend altogether? (What is $.35 + $.15?)
4. How many six-packs did Sam carry home? (How many times does 6 go into 24?)

5. How much time will it take for Karen and Linda, working together, to finish the job? (The answer is that it should take them less than two hours. It is surprising how many students in the higher grades do not realize the simple logical fact that the answer to this type of question should always be less than the least amount of time mentioned for an individual in the problem.)

Lesson 32, Pages 74–75

1. Fact (a) Length is 24 feet
   Fact (b) Width is 14 feet.
2. Fact (a) The carpet is 9 feet by 9 feet
   Fact (b) The room is 25 feet by 25 feet
3. Fact (a) The rate (speed) of the bus is 60 m.p.h.
   Fact (b) The distance from Boston to New York is 240 miles
4. Fact (a) The sandwich cost $3.25.
   Fact (b) The milk cost $.75.
5. Fact (a) 24 cans of tomato juice
   Fact (b) In six-packs
6. Fact (a) It takes Linda three hours.
   Fact (b) It takes Karen two hours.
   (The answer is, of course, less than two hours.)
7. Fact (a) Width is 10 feet.
   Fact (b) Length is 16 feet.
8. Fact (a) Up five floors
   Fact (b) Down three floors
   Fact (c) Up one floor
9. Fact (a) Three ways from Tom's house to Dick's house
   Fact (b) Five ways from Dick's house to Jane's house
   The answer to this is $3 \times 5 = 15$ ways. It is an example of the Fundamental Counting

Lesson 32, Pages 74–75, continued

Principle. If you would like to explore the answer to this question, the following diagram on the board is helpful.

Organized Listing now yields the answer. Possible routes are:

1. a, b, c, d, e
2. a, b, c, d, e
3. a, b, c, d, e

The generalization is that: If a job can be done in M ways and another job in N ways, the combination of the two jobs can be done in M x N ways.

10. Fact (a) Five miles east
Fact (b) Six miles north
Fact (c) Five miles west

The problem can be diagrammed on the board thus:

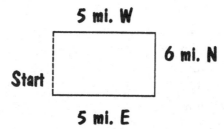

Lesson 33, Pages 76–78

1. juice	2. crying
3. school	4. frog
5. sour	6. scale
7. France	8. multiplication
9. addition	10. pound
11. question	12. nine
13. ⅞	14. .25
15. ¼	16. ½
17. ⅚ (⅔)	

Lesson 34, Pages 79–80

1. Paula jumped out of bed.
She dressed and ate breakfast in 10 minutes.
Paula ran to school.
The bell rang just as she got to the classroom.

2. The Indians dug a shallow hole.
They placed a dead fish in it.
On top of the fish they sowed the corn.
They covered the hole with soil.
The Indians waited for the sun and rain to ripen the corn.

3. The honeybee finds the flowers by following their sweet smell.
The honeybee collects the nectar and pollen.
The honeybee makes a beeline for home.
Back at the hive, she dances to tell the others where the food is.

4. Select a pattern for the dress.
Buy the fabric and thread that you need.
Cut the pattern following the directions of the pattern.
Sew the dress.

5. Break window.
Remove broken glass.
Measure window.
Buy new glass.
Install window.

6. Listen to what your teacher is asking.
Think!
Raise your hand.
Open your mouth and speak.

Lesson 35, Pages 81–82

A. We do not grow flowers in our garden.
B. **Underline:** decide on recipe, buy the ingredients needed.

Answer Key

Lesson 35, Pages 81–82, continued
Cross out: send away for a cookbook.
C. 1. Cross out: in one hour; in two hours.
   Answer: eight bushels
   2. Cross out: 30 couches in stock.
   Answer: 22 couches
   3. Cross out: $200 each; $300 each.
   Answer: 29 cows
   4. Cross out: in the last two weeks.
   Answer: lost eight
   5. Cross out: three miles; two more miles.
   Answer: 32 minutes
   6. Cross out: Judy read six; during his summer vacation.
   Answer: eight books
   7. Cross out: baseball bat costs $9.00.
   Answer: $28.00
   8. Cross out: three pounds of fresh beans; bill was $22.57; and went to the super-market.
   Answer: 10 cans
   9. Cross out: Allen got three Black Ducks, two Red Hooded Mergansers and one male Bufflehead.
   Answer: seven more birds
   10. Cross out: two walks, and held the Mustangs scoreless through six innings; team won four to one.
   Answer: 18 ÷ 9 = 2

Lesson 36, Pages 83–84

1. (b.)
2. (b.)
3. (c.)
4. (b.)
5. (c.)
6. (b.)
7. (c.) Only Rebecca or the dog could have eaten the pie. Since Rebecca was aller-gic to berries, Brittany must have had a wonderful snack.
8. (b.)
9. (c.)

	3 Speed	10 Speed	Dirt
Jose		NO	
Pedro		NO	YES
Ann		YES	

Jose must own the three-speed bike, and, thus, Ann owns the 10-speed bike.

Lesson 37, Page 85

1. six
2. 12
3. ¼
4. 12
5. 24
6. c and e
7. nine
8. 32
9. nine
10. ⅓

Lesson 38, Pages 86

1. 18 points
2. 12 plants
3. 6:30 p.m.
4. $360.00
5. Cross out: Go up nine floors; Go down six floors; Go down three floors (cancels out "Go up 9 floors" and brings you back to the first floor).
   Answer: 7th floor

 **Answer Key**

Lesson 39, Pages 87–88

A.
1. Yes (American flag)
2. No (no two the same)
3. No (American flag)
4. Yes (can't wear purple because Carlo won't wear purple)
5. Yes (American flag)
   Joey, blue; Andre, yellow; Bert, red; Kirum, brown; Carlo, white.

B. Teachers may guide students through this problem by suggesting a step-wise methodology:

First: Establish the bunk bed pairings. Which boys share a bunk bed?
Tom and Roger
Joe and Max
Pete and Dan (the only two left)

Second: Find out which set of bunk beds each pair shares: left, middle, or right (by the window).
Dan and Pete are next to the window (right).
Max and Joe are in the middle because Max sleeps between Tom and Dan.
Tom and Roger, by the method of elimination, are on the left.

Third: Determine, for each set of bunk beds, who is on the top and who is on the bottom. The conclusions are:
Roger sleeps above Tom.
Joe sleeps above Max.
Pete sleeps above Dan.

Lesson 40, Page 89

a. No (since they always fight)
b. No (Margo will starve)
c. Yes (Chico gets along with every zoo animal)
   Cage 1: Chico and Margo
   Cage 2: Bert and Daisy

Lesson 41, Page 90

1. a. Birds have feathers.
   b. The crow is a bird.
   c. A crow has feathers.
   d. True. The answer to the question is Yes.
2. A book is made up of pages.
   A dictionary has pages.
   THEN, a dictionary is a book.
   The answer to the question is Yes.

Lesson 42, Pages 93–94

A.
1. Miami and Cleveland
2. 1,374 miles
3. Boston
4. Atlanta
5. 405 miles
6. Four cities
7. About four hours
8. 1,114 (looking at the table down from Cleveland to Houston)

B.
1. $1.20
2. 2 yards x 3 feet = 6 feet x $.
3. Seven
4. $2.70
5. $.60
6. 10 feet
7. $.45

Lesson 42, Pages 93–94, continued

Some teachers might want to remind their students that one yard is equal to three feet, and that a foot is 12 inches. It will not take long before some students see the generalization of this exercise as (number of feet) x ($.30) = (cost in dollars), and they could answer the questions with the aid of the formula rather than the graph. This realization should be applauded, and the fact that graphs are geometric interpretations of algebraic formulas should be reinforced.

If you happen to have an enthusiastic class, you might even ask them questions outside the graph. For example: How much would 15 feet of ribbon cost? How much ribbon would you buy for $6.00? How much does ½ feet of ribbon cost?

The idea of "function" underlies all you do in this exercise, and when it is revisited in later classes, it will be easier to understand.

Lesson 43, Pages 95–96

1. Reading
2. Music
3. Six hours
4. 23½ hours
5. 1½ hours
6. a. math and b. language arts (3½ hrs)
   c. science and d. social studies (2½ hrs)
7. Including lunch time, the students spend 25½ hours in school. Since language arts, math, and reading account for 14 hours, they are more than half.
8. The time spent for Reading is seven hours, which is more than a quarter.

9. Twice.
10. None. The chart does not give us that information.

Lesson 44, Pages 97–98

A.
1. Elephant
2. Monkey
3. Zebra
4. Tiger
5. Order is:
   Elephant, Tiger, Zebra, Monkey

B.
1. Big Timber
2. 40 miles
3. About three hours
4. 24 miles (round-trip to Motown, then to Amity)
5. Around 4 p.m.

Lesson 45, Pages 99–100

1. ABD, ABC, DBC.
2. ABKH; HKFG; BCDK; KDEF; ACEG
3. a. Five squares
   b. Five triangles
   c. Four rectangles
   An efficient way to attack this type of counting problem is to label the regions as shown in the diagram below and then count triangular regions and squares in an organized listing.

   a and b are squares   = 2
   c + d, e + f are squares   = 2
   a + b + c + d + e + f is the big square   = 1
                                         5 squares

☞ Answer Key

Lesson 45, Pages 99–100, continued

c, d, e, f are triangles	= 4
d + e is a triangle	= 1
	5 triangles

The lesson can now be expanded to:
a + b; a + c + d; b + f + e are rectangles.
d + c is a trapezoid.

Is a + b + f a square? (No) Are there any three letters when added will give you a square? (Yes)

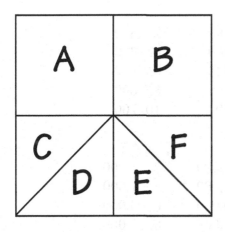

4. a. Three ways
   b. ABD and ACD
   c. AC
5. a. AB, AFB (two ways)
   b. ABE, AFE, AFBE (three ways)
   c. ABC, ABEC, AFBC, AFEC, AFBEC (five ways)
   d. Eight ways

Encourage students to look for the pattern: There is one way to get to A, that is, to start. There is one way to F, two ways to B, three ways to E, five ways to C, eight ways to D and so on, generating the sequence: 1, 1, 2, 3, 5, 8, 13, 21, and so forth, where the next term is the sum of the previous two. Thus, 13 = 8 + 5 and 21 = 13 + 8, and so forth With an enthusiastic class, you can draw a few more "blocks" on the board with the same pattern of one-way streets, and soon all students will begin to see the generalization. If you happen to remember the story of how Fibonacci discovered his famous "rabbit reproduction" sequence, you will have them jumping.

Lesson 46, Pages 101–102

1. 10 miles (7 + 3)
2. Two: Hopkington, Braintree
3. Nine: Westwood, Wellesley, Braintree, Nantasket, Rockport, Springfield, Hopkington, Cohasset, Hingham
4. 24 miles (12 x 2)
5. Six: Needham, Wellesley, Westwood, Springfield, Natick, Hopkington
6. 13 miles farther
7. Seven: Needham, Westwood, Hopkington, Wellesley, Natick, Quincy, Braintree
8. 45 miles
   Answer to riddle: MRS. EDGAR

Lesson 47, Pages 103–104

1. 12 miles
2. Three cities
3. Four cities: Mickey, Nixon, Johnson, Ford
4. Five letters (Adams)
5. 16 miles
6. Seven cities
   Answer to riddle: THE FUTURE

☞ Answer Key

Lesson 48, Page 105

	Nickels	Dimes	Quarters
1984	1	1	1
1985	1	1	1
1986		1	1
1987		1	1

He needs: 1986 nickel and 1987 nickel.

Lesson 49, Page 109

1. Differences of seven. Thus: 42, 49, 56.
2. Descending perfect squares. Thus 9, 4, 1.
3. Denominator-numerator are the same. This is an example of a "telescoping" or "collapsible" product. The next three terms will be ⅚, ⅞, ⅞. Notice that if one is asked to multiply this sequence, the answer will always be the numerator of the first term and the denominator of the last term. This problem appeared on several international mathematics exams as well as math competitions in the U.S. Encourage students to make their own "collapsible" products. They will love them because there is an easy, quick, and clever way to get the answer.
4. Going up by ½. Since the next three terms are: 3, ⅞, and 4.
5. Going up by ¼. Thus ¾, ¾, 2.

Lesson 50, Pages 110–111

1. 15

2. 2
3. 3, 2
4. 16
5. 21, 34, 55, 89, 144
6. 12   15

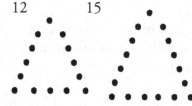

7. 17, 14, 14, 17

Lesson 51, Page 112

A.

1. 300	2. 800
3. 100	4. 300
5. 400	6. 200
7. 400	8. 600
9. 500	10. 700

B.

1. 5,000	2. 1,000
3. 6,000	4. 1,000
5. 9,000	6. 3,000
7. 5,000	8. 2,000
9. 3,000	10. 9,000

C.

1. $2.00	2. $10.00
3. $7.00	4. $9.00
5. $1.00	6. $3.00
7. $1.00	8. $3.00
9. $1.00	10. $7.00

Lesson 52, Page 113

1. About $5.00 (If they say a little below $5.00, all the better.)
2. About 400 children

Lesson 52, Page 113, continued

3. a. Yes
    b. About $2.00
    c. About $1.00
    d. About $2.00

Lesson 53, Pages 114–115

1. Around $15.00
2. 300 miles
3. 10 dozen eggs
4. About 33 rivers.
5. Eight haircuts
6. 24 books

Lesson 54, Pages 116–117

1. $.75; $.80; Super Suds
2. $100 for five days. What if it was $4.00 on Monday and then doubling every day through Friday? Students will be very surprised to see how fast numbers become big when they double every day. The classic example is: Which is bigger $1,000,000 or $1.00 doubling every day for a month?
3. Yellow cheese (at $3.25 a pound)
4. John did (in 7½ hours)
5. One penny doubling every day for a week (see No. 2, above)
6. Mr. Jones (100 is bigger than 12 x 8)
7. Red ribbon at $.79 a yard
8. Alexi got the bigger piece. (Visually)
9. Leo got the smaller piece.
10. The distances are the same. To illustrate, draw a line from D to a midpoint between AB, and a line from D to a midpoint between BC. Show that two blocks down and two to the right is the same number of blocks as one right, one down, one right, and one down.

Lesson 55, Page 118

1. a. Three
    b. Square, rectangle
    c. Three, one
    d. Two triangles and one circle.
    e. Two circles, one rectangle
    f. Six circles

2.

	.50	.25	.10	.05	
a.	1	1	1	3	= $1.00
b.	1		5		= $1.00
c.		3	2	1	= $1.00

Lesson 56, Page 119

1. Four darts in the center
2. 2(25) + 2(5)
3. 2(25) + 1(10)
4. 4(10) + 2(5) or 1(25) + 5(5)
5. 3(10) + 4(5)

    The problem is very versatile. The 5, 10, 25 circles can be used as contours to teach the students how to read a contour map. Also, one can use the 5, 10, 25 and nickel, dime, and quarter and make all sorts of money problems. For example: How could you make a dollar with four darts, and so forth.

Lesson 57, Pages 120–121

This is an exercise, drawn from real life, that attempts to explain natural phenomena. The numbers are real and force the student to concentrate on the dramatic difference between 186,000 miles per second versus 750 miles per hour! The latter speed translates to about two miles per second (750 60 60). Now, 186,000 miles per second versus two miles per second—that's amazing!

Lesson 57, Pages 120–121, continued

1. The answer to Question 1 is the speed of light, by far.
    If some students fail to see the conversion, discuss 60 m.p.h. as one mile per minute (divide by 60). Thus, one mile per second (divide by another 60).
2. Lightning. One first sees the lightning, then one hears the thunder.
3. See the lightning first.
4. One mile.
5. Three miles.
6. Five miles.
7. Going further away.

Encourage students to study the chart on page 12 a little further. They will "discover" that the longer it takes to hear the thunder, the further away both the thunder and lightning are. In fact, they are in direct proportion. Can they find the rule?

(time between lightning and thunder) = 5 (distance of lightning flash)

How natural it would be with an interested class to throw in the variables y = 5x and ask them to plug in a few values!!

Lesson 58, Page 122

2. $1 + 4 + 7 + 10 + 13 = 35$ $(14 + 14 + 7 = 35)$
3. $1 + 11 + 21 + 31 + 41 = 105$ $(42 + 42 + 21)$
4. $7 + 6 + 5 + 4 + 3 = 25$ $(10 + 10 + 5)$
5. $14 + 9 + 15 + 21 + 16 + 15 = 90$ (30×3)

6. $17 + 2 + 14 + 11 + 8 + 23 + 25 = 100$

    (4 pairs of 25 =100)

7. $47 + 62 + 33 + 13 + 8 + 17 = 180$ $(60 + 70 + 50)$
8. $1 + 2 + 3 + 4 + 5 + 6 + 7 + 8 + 9 = 45$ $(10 \times 4 + 5)$
9. $4 + 8 + 6 + 11 + 12 + 1 + 6 = 48$ (4×12)
10. $55 + 50 + 65 + 45 + 75 + 35 = 325$ $(100 + 100 + 125)$

Encourage students to find their own pairings. The idea is to teach them to look at the overall picture. Commutativity and Associativity of Addition are added bonuses.

Lesson 59, Page 123

1. $72 \div 3 = 24$ students
2. $24 \times 2 = 48$ pieces
3. $8 \times 6 = 48$, thus eight pizzas divided into six pieces each.
4. $(8 \times 7) + 8 = \$64.00$
5. $\$72 - \$64 = \$8.00$
6. Eight dollars for 24 cupcakes. About $.30 (or exactly $.33)

Lesson 60, Pages 124–125

1. $3 (\$.25) + 2 (\$.15) = \$1.05$
2. $24 \div 6 = 4$ six-packs
3. $240 \div 60 = 4$ hours
4. $[2 (85) + 2 (43)] 6 = \$1,536$
5. $14 - 6 = 8$ points
6. About 2,000

Answer Key

Lesson 61, Pages 129–130

This lesson could be done as a whole-group activity. In any case, a class discussion should precede the assignment. First, read the paragraphs aloud, then ask a volunteer to answer question No. 1. After that, students may work in pairs, individually, or as a group to complete the page. A discussion about the problem solving methods illustrated in this first lesson will be a good introduction to the book.

1. Which sessions will best help you to complete the unit?
2. and 3.
    a. Time to be spent is 1 1/2 hours.
    b. Unit will focus on shellfish and aquatic mammals.
    c. Each session is one-half hour.
4. Sessions A, C, E.
5. a. yes
    b. no
    c. yes
    d. no
    e. yes
6. The class will be able to choose three 30-minute sessions. Session A includes the elephant seal. Session C will show the habits of dolphins, sharks, and whales. Session E will discuss crabs, shrimp, and lobsters.

Lesson 62, Pages 131–132
1. b. 83
2. c. 31
3. b. 42
4. c. 51
5. a. 69
6. c. 72
7. c. 8
8. b. 6
9. a. 6
10. a. 42
    (First blouse has six choices, second blouse has six choices, and so forth … thus 7 x 6 choices.) This is a soft way to introduce the Fundamental Counting Principle: If one job can be done in M ways and another in N ways, then a combination of the two jobs can be done in M x N ways. A favorite with examiners is: If there are three ways to get from New York to Chicago and four ways to get from Chicago to Los Angeles then there are _____ ways to get from New York to Los Angeles (3 x 4).

Lesson 63, Page 133

1. a. **Main fact:** Water freezes at 32° F.

        Supporting facts: Rain turns to snow or sleet. Water on a window pane turns to frost. Surface of lakes and ponds turns to ice.
    b. Frozen water melts when the temperature rises above 32° F.
    c. **Conclusion:** It will probably snow.

2. **Main fact:** They each play a different musical instrument.

    Supporting facts: Two are wind instruments—flute and trumpet. Two are string instruments—violin and guitar. Arnold does not play the violin or flute. Kim does not play a wind instrument.

    Conclusion: Sam plays the guitar. (given)

Arnold plays trumpet (since Kim plays violin). Gertrude plays the flute (since Arnold does not play flute or violin). Kim plays the violin (no wind instrument left, and Sam plays the guitar).

(You or a volunteer might draw a chart on the board to illustrate one way to get the answer.)

Lesson 64, Page 134

1. a. **Main fact:** Vegetables grow from seeds.
    b. **Related fact:** Summer squash is a vegetable.
    c. **Then:** Squash grows from seeds.
    d. True

OR (also correct):

    a. **Main fact:** Vegetables grow from seeds.
    b. **Related fact:** Summer squash is a vegetable.
    c. **Then:** All seeds grow vegetables.
    d. False

2. Yes (IF) gerbils, hamsters, and mice are rodents, (AND) Jake is a gerbil and Holly is a hamster, (THEN) Jake and Holly are rodents.

Lesson 65, Page 135

1. ocean, sea, (or water)
2. door
3. doctor or nurse
4. car
5. den

6. surprise
7. Europe
8. globe
9. ocean
10. reptile
11. hungry
12. horizontal
13. latitude
14. y - x
15. ⅜ (= ¼)

Lesson 66, Pages 136–137

1. 0. The question, of course, states some of the unique properties of the additive identity.
2. 1. Again, some of the unique properties of the multiplicative identity.
3. 12. These problems are really wonderful. The student can work "forward" by responding to the first stimuli and make a list: 10, 11, 12, 13, 14, 15, 16, 17. The second fact eliminates all except 12 and 15. The third fact pins it down. Since the answers are given as choices, an alternative approach would be to work "backward:" The first fact eliminates suggested answers 21 and 102. The second fact eliminates 16. The third fact gives us 12 as the only choice.

    The strategies we used are:
    a. Working "forward" in a stimulus-response mode, or
    b. Working backward using the answers and arriving at a conclusion via elimination.

4. 24
5. 19

🖝 Answer Key

Lesson 66, Pages 136–137, continued

6. 30
7. 17
8. 32

Lesson 67, Page 138

1. ¼
2. ½
3. Mrs. Alfredo
4. ⅜
5. ½
6. No
7. No
8. ¼

Lesson 68, Page 139

1. 8 p.m.–12 a.m.
2. 8 a.m.–12 p.m.
3. About 18
4. After 12 noon
5. Between 4 a.m.–8 a.m. and 8 a.m.–12 p.m.
6. No. Lack of precision is a weakness in the table. (It is organized in four-hour intervals.)
7. This is to give students the experience of actually gathering the statistics and then arranging them in a meaningful way.

Lesson 69, Pages 140–141

1. Big Six News. Since it is probably the official publication of the League, it is probably reliable. Always check the source of your statistics.
2. Blames and Madhawks.
3. Blames and Bets.
4. No. The idea of introducing "negative"

answers is to make students aware of the limitations of a table. Sometimes what the chart does not say is more important than what it really says.

5. $15.00, $30.00 (Please emphasize the vocabulary of this lesson.)
6. $19.00
7. Blames at $35.00
8. Bets at $7.50
9. $58.00
10. $187.50 ÷ 6 = $31.25

Lesson 70, Pages 142–143

1.

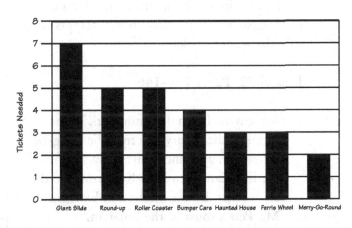

2. Pitt, Ainge, Marse, Clark, Baltic, Dors

Lesson 71, Page 144

Answers will vary, but might include:

Town Site C is not feasible, since it will probably pollute the bird sanctuary and the recreational area the town spends so much money to maintain. Town Site A is out of the question, since it is next to the shopping mall and across from the playground and school. Therefore, Town Site B is the choice.

☞ Answer Key

Lesson 71, Page 144, continued

However, a case could be made for Town Site C. Since Motown has its dump adjacent to the Green River, any pollution resulting from the dump already occurred. So why go to Town Site B and risk polluting the marsh? However, the town of Skyhook is aware of the Motown dump, yet seems determined to spend lots of money to keep that area clean for swimming, fishing, and picnicking. Thus, they would probably choose and sacrifice the marsh.

Children should see that such solutions are not clear-cut and sacrifices have to be made. Group discussions after the students' choices are handed in will bring out issues that our modern society has to face in its attempts to solve its waste problem.

Lesson 72, Pages 145–146

1. Since Mrs. Finch does not work in the art room or the library, she must be the gym instructor, and since Miss Kelly was not the librarian, then Miss Kelly must be the art teacher. By the Method of Exhaustion, Mr. Peters must be the librarian.
2. Since the jazz group has eight members and is named after an eight-sided figure, the Octagons must play jazz. Since the rock group is not named after a three-dimensional figure, they can't be the Pyramids. Moreover, the Octagons play jazz; therefore, the rock group must be the Squares. Thus, the Pyramids are the classical musicians, the only choice left.
3. Since Peter could not vote for Mack or Mike (their initials are "M"), and he could not vote for himself (in violation of club rules), he must have voted for Sam. Now,

Mack could not vote for himself or for his brother Mike, and since it is known that Sam had only one vote (Peter's), Mack voted for Peter. Mike could not vote for himself or his brother Mack, and since Sam already had a vote from Peter, Mike voted for Peter. No matter what Sam does, as long as he cannot vote for himself, Peter won the election with at least two votes. Peter could get three votes if Sam votes for him. Otherwise, Mack gets one vote or Mike gets one vote from Sam. Anyway, Peter wins the election.

4. From condition a., the quarterback wore number 7 and the running back wore number 2 (directly opposite him). Condition c. tells us that the tight end wore number 19 (he has the running back on his right) and the kicker wore number 5 opposite the tight end. Since the wide receiver was between the quarterback and tight end, he had on Number 23. Thus, the blocker wore number 17.

Lesson 73, Pages 149–150

Length	1 yd	2	3	4	5	6	7
Width	9 yds	8	7	6	5	4	3
Perimeter	20 yds (2W + 2 L)	20	20	20	20	20	20
Area (L x W)	9	16 sq. yds	21	24	25	24	21
	a.	b.	c.	d.	e.	f.	g.

1. 5 x 5
2. 1 x 9
3. square; e

The generalization for this lesson is: Given a fixed perimeter, the rectangular field with the maximum area is going to turn out to be a square. The student, by completing the table, accounts for all the whole number possibilities (guessing) and, by checking the Area row (testing), discovers the dimension that will give the maximum area. In higher mathematics, the shape that encloses the maximum area with a fixed length will turn out to be a circle. This lesson is a good introduction to maxima-minima theory.

4. A rectangle in 1:4 ratio.

5. c and g: 21 sq. yds.; d and f: 24 sq. yds. If the table was extended, we would, of course, have b = h = 16 sq. yds. and a = i = 9 sq. yds.

6. Yes. They show the "down" turn in areas, thus confirming our guess that no other "larger" areas can occur.

7. If one follows the hint, one will start with: length 1 yd, width 29 yds; length 2 yds., width 28 yds., and so forth … and discover that 15 x 15 will give the maximum area. Students who follow the hint and the structure of the lesson to come up with 15 x 15 should be applauded. It should, however, be pointed out that there is a faster way.

   Since question 1 suggests the figure giving the maximum area is a square, one can take the fixed perimeter 60, divide by 4, (sides of a square are always equal, thus each side must be 15), and multiply 15 x 15 to get the maximum area: 225 sq. yds. Once the above method is either discovered by a student or suggested by the teacher, several other examples should follow, thus reinforcing the generalization of the entire lesson.

8. The square root of 81 is 9, and 4 x 9 = 36. Also, one can set it up as: L = W in a square, thus L x L = 81 and L = 9.

Therefore, the perimeter is 9 x 4 = 36 yds. of fencing.

Lesson 74, Pages 151–152

7 lb. bags	Cost per bag	Total Cost	3 lb. bags	Cost per bag	Total Cost	Total in lbs.	TOTAL COST
4	$4.25	$17.00	0	$2.39	0	28	$17.00
3	$4.25	$12.75	1	$2.39	$2.39	24	$15.14
2	$4.25	$8.50	3	$2.39	$7.17	23	$15.67
1	$4.25	$4.25	6	$2.39	$14.34	25	$18.59

A good first guess would be four 7-lb. bags (28 lbs.). After completing the table above one can see that the combination of three 7-lb. bags and one 3-lb. bag costs the least, at $15.14. Buying 24 lbs. of cement is less expensive than buying 23 lbs. under the terms of this sale. Students will find that surprising, and an important lesson in consumerism will be learned.

1. 23 lbs.
2. $17.00
3. 28 lbs.
4. 21 lbs.
5. three lbs.
6. 24 lbs.
7. $15.14
8. Two 7-lb bags and three 3-lb bags
9. $15.67
10. No. It is the most expensive, at $18.59.
11. The best combination: three 7-lb bags and one 3-lb. bag.

Lesson 75, Page 153

A student might have trouble starting this problem. You could help out by asking: Could Ellie have bought all angelfish? (No, since that would cost $7.00.) Could she have bought all goldfish? (No, since that would cost $4.48.)

Lesson 75, Page 153, continued

Thus, she must have bought a combination. Could Ellie have bought 10 angelfish? No. Because if she did, she would have spent $5.00 and she could not buy four goldfish with the additional $.56. Thus, she must have bought less than 10 angelfish—say, 9.

Angelfish $0.50		Goldfish $0.32		TOTALS	
Number	Cost	Number	Cost	Number	Cost
9	$4.50	5	$1.60	14	$6.10
8	$4.00	6	$1.92	14	$5.92
7	$3.50	7	$2.24	14	$5.74
6	$3.00	8	$2.56	14	$5.56
5	$2.50	9	$2.88	14	$5.38

After completing the table, one can see that if Ellie spent $5.56 and bought 14 fish at the above prices, she must have bought six angelfish for a total of $3.00 and eight goldfish for a total of $2.56.

Lesson 76, Page 154

1. Counterclockwise starting at 12 o'clock: 2, 4, 3, 1, with 5 in the middle. This activity is versatile. One could ask, for example, how to arrange numbers to give the sum of eight. Again counterclockwise starting at 12 o'clock: 4, 2, 3, 5, with 1 in the middle. For a sum of nine, counterclockwise as above: 1, 2, 5, 4, with 3 in the middle.
2. Starting at a vertex and going in a counterclockwise direction: 1, 6, 2, 4, 3, 5.
3. 12
4. 17
5. 64
6. 5½
7. 1⅞
   The underlying idea of the above is, of course, the introduction of the unknown "x" and solving the equation.

For example, in #3:
$$3x + 16 = 52$$
$$3x + 16 - 16 = 52 - 16 \quad \text{(Subtract 16 from both sides)}$$
$$3x = 36 \quad \text{(doing the arithmetic)}$$
and $x = 12$ (division by 3)

During a discussion of the lesson, one might ask if there is a more "sure" way to do problems 3–7 without resorting to a "Guess and Test" strategy, which could be cumbersome.

With an enthusiastic class, the variable "x" can be introduced in place of the "square" and a discussion of how to solve linear equations might ensue.

Notice on question 6 that both a Guess and Test strategy as well as the more formal setting up of the equation will lead to the answer, but they are <u>not</u> the most efficient way to do the problem. Since the possible answers are given, a "Working Backward" approach eliminates almost all possibilities except 5½. Estimate the problem as: $3 \times \square = 19$. Then 8 and 7 are too big (24 and 21 respectively). Similarly 4½ and 3 are too small (13½ and 9 respectively), leaving 5½ as the most reasonable answer.

Lesson 77, Pages 155–156

1.
   a. 50—Each term is half of the preceding.

   b. ⬡ hexagon

Answer Key

c. ⁹⁄₁₀
d. 16
e. Bush
f. 38 (up by 9)
g. 13—Each term is the sum of the preceding two. (Fibonacci)
h. 26 (increase interval by two each time)
i.

If the first three circles of the question indicate the first, second, and third quadrants respectively, then the last two show the fourth and back to the first.

2. A = 60 (30, 6)
3. 210, 70, 35, 7, 5
4.

# sides		# diagonals	
3		0	2
4		2	
5		5	3
6		9	4
•		14	5
•		20	6
•		27	7
•		35	8
•		34	9
12		44	10

The last column gives us the difference between the number of diagonals of two consecutive figures. By completing the difference column, we arrive at 44 as the number of diagonals in a dodecagon. By extending the pattern, we could find the diagonals of any polygon.

Lesson 78, Pages 157–158

This and the next lesson are probably best done as a group activity with guided instruction. The elegance of the pattern repetition will amaze and delight your students. The lessons may be also given in conjunction with, or as follow-up to, the use of such manipulatives as geo-boards or pattern blocks.

4th	15	$(5 + 4 + 3 + 2 + 1)$
5th	21	$(6 + 5 + 4 + 3 + 2 + 1)$
6th	28	$(7 + 6 + 5 + 4 + 3 + 2 + 1)$
7th	36	$(8 + 7 + 6 + 5 + 4 + 3 + 2 + 1)$

1. two dots
2. three dots; four dots
3. 11 dots
4. n + 1; 754 dots (Reinforce the pattern with students: triangle number + 1 = number of dots on each side)
5. three dots
6. six dots (The pattern repeats itself)
7. 5th triangle number; 21 dots
8. (n - 3) triangle number (The pattern is established.)
9. 647th
10. In the 3, 4, 5, 6 … sequence

Lesson 79, Page 159

4-square	16	(4 x 4)	4 □ (4^2)
5-square	25	(5 x 5)	5 □ (5^2)
6-square	36	(6 x 6)	6 □ (6^2)

1. $50 \times 50 = 2{,}500$ (50^2)
2. 100 dots on each side
3. a. eight dots
   b. 12 dots
   c. 16 dots
   d. 20 dots

Lesson 79, Page 159, continued

4. 24 dots

5. 36 dots. The generalization is (n - 1) x 4 = the number of dots around the perimeter of n-square.

Lesson 80, Page 160

5-square	3^2
6-square	4^2
7-square	5^2

1. 48^2 (48 x 48 = 2304)
2. $(n-2)^2$ ((n - 2) (n - 2))
3. $(748)^2$ (559, 504)

Lesson 81, Pages 161–162

(A review of geometric shapes would be a useful introduction to this lesson and the next one on Tiling.)

A. Mexican Hat Triangle Problem
If we name the regions M, E, X, I, C, O, as indicated in the diagram, then:

1. E, X, I, C, O - 5 in all
2. E + X; X + I; I + C; C + O; M + C; M + X- 6 in all
3. E + X + I; I + C + O - 2 in all
4. M + X + I + C + O - just 1
5. None
6. Thus, the total number of triangles in the Mexican Hat is 14 (5 + 6 + 2 + 1).

The lesson forces the students not to just look at a diagram, but actually to see what's in it. It reinforces the fact that geometric figures—in this case triangles—are independent of size. Large or small, they

are all triangles. The introduction of suitable notation is of immense importance in mathematics since it enables our solution to be presented in a precise and logical manner that anyone can understand. Students must learn to write math down in an orderly fashion. Notice also that, by the way we have solved the problem using the introduced notation, we are sure we got all the triangles in the figure. Obviously there are no six-region or seven-region triangles. All possibilities have been accounted for.

B. Star Triangle Problem
Obviously, notations will vary. If we name the different regions of the star as indicated in the following figure then:

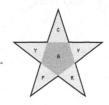 

1. one-region triangles:
   c, y, p, r, u - 5 in all
2. two-region triangles:
   none
3. three-region triangles:
   c + s + p; c + s + r; u + s + y; u + s + p; y + s + r-5 in all
4. four-region triangles:
   none
5. Therefore, the total number of triangles in the star is 10.

Lesson 82, Pages 163–164

1. three square units

Lesson 82, Pages 163–164, continued

2. 12 units long

3. (a) four square units, 10 units long

4. 26 square units

5. yes ⊞ Both have perimeter eight.

6. Answers will vary. One of them could be

—as long as the new tile has one side in common with the Figure 3.

7.

Tile must have three sides in common with Figure 3.

8. a. No, since she must start with one tile and it has perimeter four.

b. No, since from perimeter four one can only go to perimeter six. The tile will have only one side in common with the original tile.

c. No, since from perimeter six one can only go to eight if one adds a tile. There is no way to go up in perimeter by one.

d. No. The generalization is this: As you go up one tile then (old perimeter - 1) + 3 = new perimeter.

9. Never. (Even - 1) + 3 = always even.

10. Even numbers

11. a. increases; two

b. stays the same or is unchanged

c. decreases; two

12. Yes. Yes. Area will always increase by one as you add a tile.

(Math manipulatives are excellent working tools for this lesson.) Tiling is an absolutely wonderful activity. You can do it with squares, equilateral triangles, hexagons, and so forth, and have students investigate several aspects of the polyominoes. In this lesson, we chose tiling squares and kept track of the area and perimeter. The questions in the lesson are given in a sequence that might occur in the mind of a curious youngster as he or she goes through the activity. One might also use the questions as guided instruction. They lead to generalizations that the students discover as they progress through the lesson. Students find it amazing that one can add a tile to a polyomino and the perimeter will be less than what it was before. That perimeters can only be even numbers and that the area always goes up by one as a tile is added are conjectures that result from this lesson. The activity is not only manipulative, but also geometric. By seeing the visual element in the picture, the student learns a very important lesson in problem solving: If you can draw a picture or diagram, it will be easier to solve a problem.

Notice that this lesson introduces a new word: *polyomino*. We define it as an arrangement of tiles with common edges. The tiles could be squares, triangles, or any other geometric figure we choose .It has been a favorite problem of examiners to give a definition that the student has never seen before and ask several questions concerning the definition to see whether the student has understood its meaning. By exposing our students to this type of question, we substantially lower their anxiety when they encounter something similar on one of our national exams.

☞ Answer Key

Lesson 83, Pages 167–168

1. blue-blue   blue-green
    blue-red   white-blue
    white-green   white-red

    six combinations (2 x 3)

2. computers-Army   mechanics-Army
    economics-Army   computers-Navy
    mechanics-Navy   economics-Navy
    computers-Air Force   mechanics-Air Force
    economics-Air Force   computers-Marines
    mechanics-Marines   economics-Marines

    12 combinations (3 x 4)

3. ham-milk   peanut butter-milk
    bologna-milk   ham-cocoa
    peanut butter-cocoa   bologna-cocoa
    ham-apple juice   peanut butter-apple juice
    bologna-apple juice   ham-lemonade
    peanut butter-lemonade   bologna-lemonade
    turkey-milk   tuna-milk
    turkey-cocoa   tuna-cocoa
    turkey-apple juice   tuna-apple juice
    turkey-lemonade   tuna-lemonade

    20 combinations (5 x 4)

4. 48 combinations (8 x 6)

Lesson 84, Pages 169–170

1. c.
2. b.
3. a.
4. a. 7:12
    b. 3:4
5. a. 9.25:10 (or 37:40)
    b. Sterling. Oriental silver is only 4:5.
6. a. 3:1

b. two cans
c. 2 ÷ 1/2 = 4 x 3 = 12 cans of water.

7. a. 1:5
    b. $2.50
    c. Lisa collects $.20 on the dollar, thus Lisa kept $4.00 of the $20.00 she collected.
    d. 100 x .25 = $25.00. If she kept one in five she must have kept $5.00 and returned $20.00 to the company at the end of the week.

Lesson 85, Pages 171–172

1. b. 2: (2 x 2) 2: 4
    c. 4: (4 x 4) 4: 16
    d. 8: (8 x 8) 8: 64
    We can conclude that: If you double the Side of the square, then you increase the Area x 4 (quadruple the Area).
2. a. Assuming Saturdays and Sundays off plus holidays (12), the ratio is 3:5 (18:30 in lowest terms).
    b. 2:5 (12:30 in lowest terms)
    c. 1:6 (3:18 reduced)
    d. 2:3 (12:18 reduced)

Lesson 86, Page 173

1. snow in January
2. when you do homework
3. three-choice quiz (33% versus 20%)
4. average .169
5. college graduate
6. card with hearts (13 hearts, only 4 queens)
7. vowel (seven vowels, only one P)
8. seagull
9. U.S. President
10. 3/5 probability

Lesson 87, Page 174

1. None. Zero.
2. Absolutely certain or definite. One.

The main purpose of the above two questions is to establish the limits of probability. In other words, the probability of an event ranges from 0 (never happens) to 1 (sure thing). Since all other probabilities lie in between, it follows that the probability of an event is a fraction.

3. a. A black ball (4 black balls and only 2 white balls)
   b. P (white ball)= 2/6 = 1/3
   c. P (blackball) = 4/6 = 2/3
4. One in two or 1:2, 1/2

Lesson 88, Pages 175–176

1. a. A girl's name
   b. 3/8   c. 5/8
   d. Name that begins with S
   e. 1   f. 1/4
   g. 1/8

2. a. 16 out of 320 or 16:320 or 1:20 (1/20)
   b. 32 out of 320 or 1:10 (1/10)
   c. 1. It will be a sure thing.
   d. $20.00. You have to buy all 320 players at 16 for $1.00. Thus, 320:16 = 20 x 1 = 20
3. 50/50; 50/100 or 1/2

Lesson 89, Pages 177–178

(You might want to ask students to construct a spinner for this activity—or bring one

from a board game.)
1. 1:6 or 1/6   2. 1/6
3. 1/3   4. 1/2
5. Very, very small. It will really be zero.
6. 2/3   7. 1/3
8. 1 (adding probabilities) 9. 1
10. 3:6 or 3/6 or 1/2
11. 3:6 or 3/6 or 1/2
12. 6:6 or 6/1 or 1:1 or 1/1

Lesson 90, Pages 179–180

This lesson is included as an extension activity for challenged and enthusiastic students.

2. Multiplying the first and last numbers yields 1, and so forth. Following this hint, the answer is
   1 (1/4 x 4 = 1; 1/3 x 3 = 1, etc.)
3. The questions says: "How far apart are they when they meet?" The distance between them will be zero miles.
4. An 8 x 8 checkerboard has 64 unit squares. The one with coordinates (4, 4) is the last one, #64. Back up two, you are in the 0 at 62.
5. By "flipping" the IV quadrant from right to left, you have one-half of the circle shaded.
6. If you were to divide the big square with a horizontal line and a vertical line into four equal squares, you could see that each one has half of its area shaded. Hence, half of the main square is shaded.
7. One "outside" triangle cancels one "shaded" triangle. There is still one "outside" triangle left. Thus, the L-shaped figure has more area.
8. 1/8. The two triangles with edges AF and CD form another square.